Quilts for Kids

Carolann M. Palmer

That Patchwork Place®

Dedication

A special word of dedication and thanks to my daughters, who have provided the "little reasons" for this book, and to the "reasons," who have now acquired their first big bed to make room for little brother or sister. Thanks Carolee, Lorellen, and Jan.

Credits

Editor . . . . Barbara Weiland
Managing Editor . . . . Greg Sharp
Copy Editor . . . . Liz McGehee
Text and Cover Design . . . . Judy Petry
Typesetting . . . . Laura Jensen
Photography . . . . Brent Kane
Illustration and Graphics . . . . . . Karin LaFramboise
Barb Tourtillotte

Quilts for Kids©
©1993 by Carolann M. Palmer

That Patchwork Place, Inc.
PO Box 118, Bothell, WA 98041-0118 USA

Printed in the United States of America
98 97 96 95 94 93   6 5 4 3 2 1

Library of Congress Cataloging-in-Publication Data
Palmer, Carolann.
    Quilts for kids/by Carolann M. Palmer.
        p. cm.
    ISBN 1-56477-036-2:
        1. Quilting —Patterns. 2. Patchwork—Patterns.
    3. Appliqué—Patterns. 4. Childrens's quilts.
    I. Title
    TT835.P354 1993
    746.9'7—dc20   93-15933
                                                    CIP

Acknowledgments

A bouquet of sincere thanks to each of the pattern testers, who have given of their time, energy, and sometimes frustration to see that you have accurate patterns to follow. Thanks go to: Arlene Sheckler, Judy Pollard, Joyce Miller, Marjorie Meyers, Bunnie Johanson, Joan Dawson, Deann Thompson, Diane Roubal, Delayne LaVallie, Pat Marquardt, Peg Storey, Eloise Strain, Martha Ahern, Barbara Markham, Bev Bodine, Nancy Chong, and Nancy Ewell.

Contents

Preface

Making baby quilts has always been a source of enjoyment for me. Through the years, I've given away at least one hundred and fifty of them to friends and relatives, and I'm still making them. What fun it was

when my first grandchild arrived! I made Anthony a very special quilt before his birth and, of course, after he was born, I had to make one especially for him with his name on it in a design a boy would treasure. When he turned two, he had to have a Christmas quilt in keeping with the season for cold December nights. He came to me one day, not long after his little brother had arrived, and said, "Grandma, I'm in a big bed now and I need a bigger quilt."

As more grandchildren arrived, I realized that although babies usually take nine months to arrive, grandchildren can come in batches. As a result, I'm still making quilts for all of them— and I love it. Before you know it, I'll be making quilts for high school graduation gifts! Seven grandchildren do keep me busy.

When planning quilts for kids' first big beds, I wanted to use designs that would interest a growing child, not a baby. And, I didn't want to make quilts that were scaled-down versions of typically adult designs. The quilt patterns presented here are the result of this thought process. I hope you will enjoy each one.

Caralann M. Palmer

Introduction

The designs in this book are based on things that are familiar to children. For example, "Dream Wardrobe" was designed for little girls who love to play with paper dolls or dream of having beautiful dresses. An alternate pattern for a boy's wardrobe is also included. Airplanes, boats, snails, and frogs delight children of all ages. Cats are a universal favorite and are the subject of "Dream Chaser." When you turn this quilt upside down, you'll find a whole litter of gray kitties in the tessellated design.

I've included quilts in a variety of sizes, including five with instructions for crib quilts, just in case you need to make a baby quilt. Some are appropriate for wall hangings. Wind Spinner, Dream Wardrobe, Rainsong, or Bird Garden might find their home above a bed, while Flying High, Dream Chaser, Dancing Snails, and Frog Pond are amply sized to cover a twin-size bed. Select your child's favorite, then make it as it is, make more blocks to make it larger, or rearrange the blocks to fit a special bed.

The first section of this book contains basic techniques to help you have a successful quilting experience. The right tools, quick techniques, and fabric-selection guidelines are included. For a change, try something different, evaluate it, incorporate it into your quilting skills if you like it, or toss it out if you don't. Finishing directions are also included.

Patterns for thirteen different quilt designs follow the basic techniques. Use the full-color photo of the quilt you are making as a guide when selecting fabrics and making your own version.

Have a great time as you make a quilt for that special child in your life.

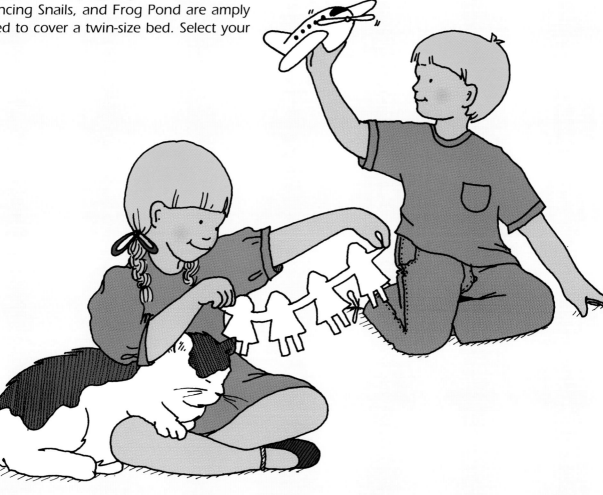

Selecting Fabric

There are several important things to remember when choosing fabric for a child's quilt.

✎ Choose one fabric you can't live without, then select fabrics that blend with the colors in the first fabric.

✎ Choose fabrics that provide visual texture as well as contrast.

✎ Choose a light, a medium, and a dark fabric from one or two color families.

✎ Trust your eye to tell you what looks best to you. When making quilts for children, start with a fabric or fabrics that remind you of the design subject. For instance, finding greens for frogs, or fabric that looks like kitten fur or bird feathers, may get you started. In Flying High (page 16), the cloud background was an obvious place to begin; then came the bright prints for the planes. For the sashing in Windsails (page 36) and Frog Pond (page 74), I wanted underwater prints to set the tone. Many of the quilts in this book include a variety of prints, which adds sparkle and interest.

✎ Children like bright, clear colors and lots of them. Choose a variety of large and small prints, stripes, dots, and diagonally printed fabrics. Look for interesting novelty prints, perhaps with a theme that appeals to the child for whom you are making the quilt—sewing tools for a budding seamstress, basketballs for sports fans, or cats for the cat lover.

✎ It is easiest to work with fabrics made of 100% cotton. Cotton takes dye evenly and is easy to press.

After you have selected the quilt you want to make, go to your local quilt shop and take a slow stroll to see what is available before you begin the fabric-selection process. Select that one special fabric and then build a collection of coordinating fabrics around it, following the guidelines above. A word of caution: It is best not to mention to anyone that you are looking for frog eyes or bird wings.

Preshrink all fabric in a basin of warm water to remove all excess dye. Rinse until water is clear, then dry fabric and press. This last step is essential. Some quilters machine wash their fabrics, but I recommend hand washing so you can monitor the color of the rinse water. You don't want to include in your quilt any fabrics that are going to run and fade onto other fabrics. Yardage requirements are based on a usable width of 42". If, after preshrinking, your fabric is not at least 42" wide, you may need additional yardage for the quilt.

Assembling Tools

There are many quilting tools available to speed the process of making accurately cut and pieced quilts. Following are the basic tools you need to make the quilts in this book.

Scissors: A pair of fabric scissors is a must. Use them only for cutting fabric. Put a padlock on them if necessary, or hide them in a secret place so no one else can use them. Paper scissors are also essential. Keep both sharpened and in a safe place, where little fingers can't reach them easily.

Rotary Cutter: A rotary cutter makes quick and easy work of accurately cutting the pieces for your quilt. It looks like a pizza cutter, has a super sharp blade, and cuts through several layers at once with ease. You will also need a self-healing rotary cutting mat and ruler.

Rulers: Clear acrylic rulers marked in ⅛" increments are essential for rotary cutting. My favorites are the 6" Bias Square® and a 6" x 12" ruler. Other sizes are available at your local quilt shop and are definite sanity savers for quilters.

Needles: Use the proper one for each process in quilting. Hand sewing, appliqué,

and quilting needles are good starters. A soft-sculpture needle is especially good for hand basting quilt layers together.

Pins: Special long quilters' pins are essential for pinning together the quilt layers for basting. They are also handy for regular sewing use.

Thimble: Thimbles are available in metal, leather, or plastic and come in a variety of shapes and sizes. Find one that fits your finger comfortably. Try several and find the style that suits you best.

Markers: Markers are available in a variety of types, including felt-tip markers, pens, pencils, and chalk in all shapes, colors, and sizes. Make sure that the marker you use is designed for quilting, and test before use to make sure marks are removable.

Iron: A good steam iron is a must, along with a well-padded ironing board. You may want to put padding on a hollow-core door to create a large pressing surface.

Sewing Machine: Buy the best you can afford that meets your needs. For basic quilting, you need one with good stitch quality—even, balanced stitches with no puckering or pulling. Have it serviced at least once a year to keep it in good working order.

Rotary Cutting

Accuracy is important in every step of making a quilt, but especially in cutting the pieces from the fabric. An inaccuracy of only ¹⁄₁₆" on each block grows to 1" after sewing eight seams, causing serious construction problems, especially if your quilt is large.

Directions for the quilts in this book are written for rotary cutting, because the rotary cutter makes it easy to accurately cut the pieces for your quilt—and to do it quickly. First, you cut long strips of fabric from

selvage to selvage. Then you cut the strips into squares and triangles, eliminating the use of templates.

If using a rotary cutter for the first time, follow the manufacturer's safety precautions. The following instructions will help you get started. You will need a rotary cutter, self-healing rotary-cutting mat, and a straight-edge rotary ruler, available at your local quilt shop.

How to Rotary Cut Strips and Squares

1. Press preshrunk fabric with selvages matching. Fold in half again, lengthwise. You now have four layers.
2. Align a square ruler with the fold of the fabric and place a cutting ruler to the left. Remove the square and cut, rolling the cutter away from you, across the fabric, along the edge of the ruler.

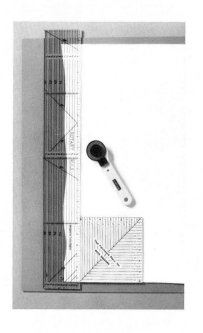

3. Cut fabric into strips, in the widths given in the quilt pattern you are following.

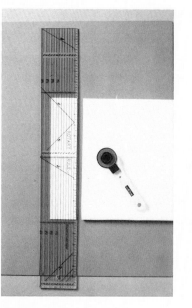

Then cut the strip into squares the width of the strip.

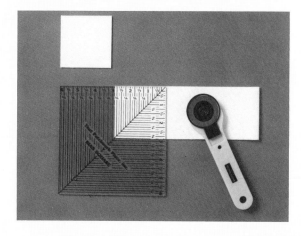

Sometimes you will be directed to cut the squares diagonally to create two half-square triangles or to cut twice diagonally to create four quarter-square triangles.

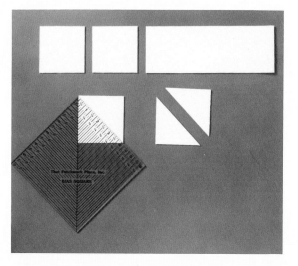

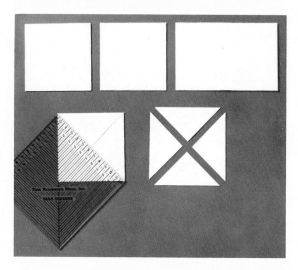

4. Cut bias strips by positioning the ruler at a 45° angle to the selvage edge. Make all cuts parallel to the first cut.

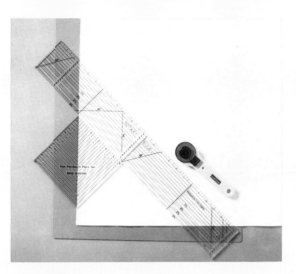

If the position of the fabric or straight edge is uncomfortable for you, reverse it. You should not feel like a pretzel or have to stand on your head to rotary cut. Practice on some scrap fabric and soon you will have this technique mastered.

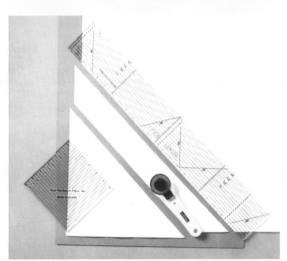

How to Rotary Cut and Assemble Half-Square Triangle Units

1. Cut squares the size given in the quilt pattern of your choice. (The size of the square is determined by adding ⅞" to the desired finished size of one short side of the triangle.)

2. Pair two contrasting squares with right sides together.
3. Draw a diagonal line from corner to corner on the wrong side of the lightest-colored square.
4. Stitch ¼" away from the drawn line on both sides.
5. Cut on the line between rows of stitching and press the seams to one side of each piece, making two half-square triangle units.

Draw a line.   Stitch and cut.   2 half-square triangle units

6. Square up the block to the desired finished size plus ½" for seam allowances (¼" on each side). For example, a 2" finished square should measure 2½" square before sewing it to other pieces in the quilt top.

How to Rotary Cut Trapezoids

1. Cut a fabric strip in the width given in the quilt pattern you are following.
2. Make a cut at a 45°-angle at the left end of the strip as shown.

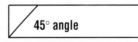

45° angle

3. Using the trapezoid measurement given in the quilt pattern, measure along the bottom edge of the strip and position the ruler so you can make a 45°-angle cut in the opposite direction.
4. Continue cutting trapezoids across the strip, alternating the direction of each cut as shown.

Continue across strip...

How to Cut and Sew Quick Geese

1. Cut rectangles and squares in the sizes given in the quilt pattern you've chosen.
2. Draw a diagonal line from corner to corner on the back of each square.
3. Position a square on one end of a rectangle.
4. Sew on the line and trim away the outer corner, ¼" away from the stitching line.
5. Flip up the resulting triangle and press.
6. Repeat on the opposite side of the rectangle.

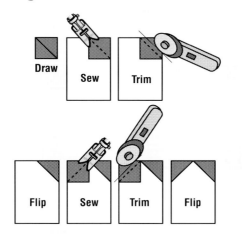

Templates

Several quilts require templates and these can be found with the quilt patterns. Each template is identified by the quilt name and a template letter. Cutting directions indicate the number of pieces to cut from each fabric. Several templates are labeled "Cut 1 and 1r," which means to cut a specified number with the template face up, then flip it over and cut the specified number in reverse. To make it easier, fold fabric wrong sides together and cut only once, using the template. This yields 2 pieces that are mirror images of each other.

All templates include a ¼"-wide seam allowance as do the border cutting directions, except where noted. Grain line is noted where needed.

Helpful Hint

Before trimming in step 4, above, stitch ½" from first stitching, toward the outer corner; then cut between the two lines of stitching. You will have a small half-square triangle left over from each corner. Save them to use in a doll quilt, potholder, or pillow.

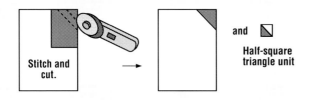

Appliqué

Appliqué is used on some of the quilts in this book. You may appliqué by hand or machine. I prefer a technique called paper piecing.

Paper–Pieced Appliqué

1. Trace and cut appliquéd pattern pieces from construction paper. Do not add seam allowances.
2. Place paper piece on wrong side of fabric and pin. Cut, adding a ¼" allowance all around as you cut.

Pin paper to fabric.

3. Fold the ¼" allowance over the edge of the paper piece and baste to the paper, using a running stitch and sewing through the paper. Do not use knots or backstitches since the basting stitches and paper must be removed in a later step.

Baste fabric to paper, sewing through paper.

4. Clip inner curves and corners as needed. On outer curves, ease in fullness, using a small running stitch to gather the fabric. Do not sew through the paper on outer curves. The basting stitches through the paper on either end of the outer curve hold the fabric to the paper.

Ease in fullness on curves with small running stitch.

5. Press all fabric pieces, making sure that all edges are smooth and free of lumps and bumps and unwanted "points."

6. Appliqué fabric pieces to the background, using a small blind stitch and matching thread. Stitches should be about ⅛" apart. When appliqué is completed, turn to wrong side and carefully cut away the fabric behind the appliquéd piece, leaving ¼" allowance of fabric inside the stitching. Remove the basting thread from the appliqué, and the paper will come out easily. Trimming the background fabric in this manner leaves one less fabric layer to quilt.

Blindstitch fabric to background.

Interfaced Appliqué

Try interfaced appliqué for the fans in Fanfleur (page 53) and the parasols in Rainsong (page 32). Machine stitch segments together; then use the pieced unit as a pattern to cut a piece of lightweight interfacing to match. With right sides together, stitch the interfacing to the pieced unit along the outer curved edge. Turn and press; then machine stitch to the quilt block with invisible thread. Interface and appliqué fan centers in the same way.

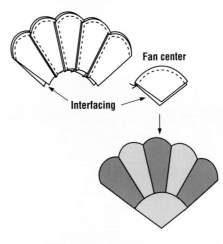

Fan center

Interfacing

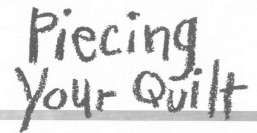

Piecing Your Quilt

Just as accuracy is important when cutting quilt pieces, it is also vital when sewing the pieces together to make the blocks and when sewing the blocks together to complete the quilt top. All seam allowances are ¼" wide so it is important to establish a ¼"-wide seam-allowance mark on your sewing machine in some form. Do not assume the line on your throat plate is exactly ¼" from the point of the needle.

One way to mark an accurate seam guide is to place masking tape on the throat plate exactly ¼" from the needle. Use three or four layers to build up the tape so it will guide the fabric, or use a piece of adhesive-backed moleskin, which is available in drugstores. You may need to cut the tape so it fits around the feed dog.

To ensure stitching accuracy, it's also helpful to use the built-in, even-feed or attachment feature on your machine. Consult your machine manual for directions.

Pressing

Always press from the right side of the fabric to avoid pleats at the seam line. Press each seam before adding another piece with a seam that crosses it. When pressing bias edges, be careful not to stretch and distort them. Press seams away from where you plan to quilt, to avoid stitching through bulky layers.

When in doubt about which way to press seams, look at each block and the quilt top as a whole, then decide how to press. By taking time to plan carefully at this stage of construction, you can eliminate hard bumps within the blocks and at points where the blocks are joined together, and your seam intersections will be easier to match up.

Finishing Your Quilt

Mark the Quilt Top

First decide on a quilting design and mark it onto the quilt top. Most of the quilts in this book were quilted by stitching "in-the-ditch"—in or close to the seam lines. This doesn't require any marking. Some of the quilting designs were marked onto the top with a marker. I tested the marker on fabric first to make sure the marks could be removed easily. I used ¼"-wide masking tape to mark other designs.

I machine quilted some of the more intricate border designs very quickly by first tracing them onto narrow strips of tracing paper cut the length of each border. I pinned the paper to the border, then stitched with invisible thread, following the quilting design on the paper. The paper tore away easily once the quilting was completed but held up well for quilting a border design with three or four design lines. This method works especially well on dark-colored borders, where it is often difficult to mark quilting lines dark enough to see easily.

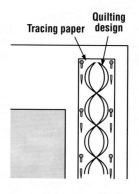

Tracing paper   Quilting design

Assemble the Layers

1. Cut batting and prepare the backing, making them both 2"–4" larger than the finished quilt top all around.

2. With the wrong side up, tape the backing to the floor or a large table, using masking tape and making sure the piece is smooth and taut and free of wrinkles. Place batting on top of backing and smooth out. Carefully place the quilt top, right side up, on batting, making sure the backing and batting extend beyond the top all around. Working from the center out, smooth with hands.

3. Starting at the center of the quilt, pin all three layers together with quilting pins. Pin at 4"–6" intervals across the quilt surface. Smooth out with hands before adding each pin.

4. Starting at the center and working out, baste quilt layers together in a grid, with rows spaced 4"–6" apart over the entire quilt surface. Smooth out with hands as needed. Do not trim the excess batting and backing until after binding is attached. If the batting is in the way while you quilt, turn the edge of the backing over the batting to the front of the quilt and baste in place temporarily.

Quilt It!

Now you're ready to quilt. I machine quilted most of the quilts in this book with invisible nylon quilting thread. I find this method quick and very practical, especially for kids' quilts, which often get lots of hard wear. I use the even-feed feature on my machine to help feed the fabric through smoothly, eliminating unwanted puckers and pleats on the underside of the quilt. If your machine doesn't have a built-in, even-feed feature, you may be able to purchase an even-feed attachment from your dealer. It's worth checking.

If you prefer to quilt by hand, place your prepared quilt in a hoop or on a quilt frame. To quilt, start at the center and stitch out to the edges, moving the hoop or frame as needed. Using quilting thread and a quilting needle, take tiny running stitches, checking the back of the quilt frequently to be sure the needle goes all the way through the batting and the backing. Remember to quilt around the part of the design you want to stand out most, to give it an added dimension.

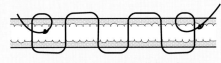

Be sure stitches go through all three layers.

If you prefer to tie your quilt, use embroidery floss, pearl cotton, or lightweight yarn. With double thread, stitch and tie square knots at 6" intervals across the surface of the quilt.

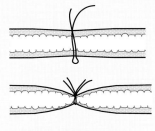

Tying is another option.

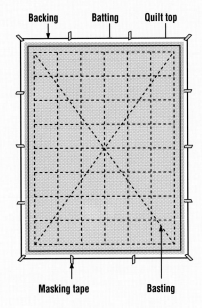

Backing   Batting   Quilt top

Masking tape   Basting

Bind the Edges

I prefer bias binding cut and pieced from the binding fabric I've chosen.

To cut bias for binding:

1. Fold the fabric by bringing the selvage edge to meet a straightened edge of the fabric. Press. Cut carefully on the pressed fold. This cut edge is bias.

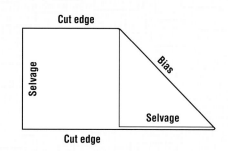

2. Measure and cut 2½"-wide bias strips parallel to the cut edge.

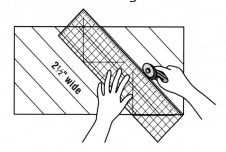

3. Using diagonal seams, join strips into one long piece of binding. Press seams open.

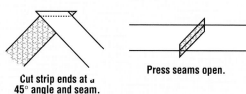

Cut strip ends at a 45° angle and seam.   Press seams open.

4. At one end of the binding, turn under and press ¼" at a 45° angle as shown. Then fold in half lengthwise, wrong sides together, with raw edges matching. Press lightly.

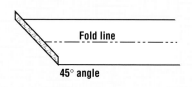

Fold line

45° angle

To attach bias binding:

1. Beginning in the center of one side of the quilt, align the raw edges of the binding with the raw edges of the quilt top.
   Note: The batting and backing should still extend beyond the edges of the quilt.

2. Stitch the binding to the quilt top, using a ¼"-wide seam allowance and stopping exactly ¼" from the first corner. Backstitch and remove from machine.

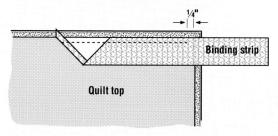

3. Fold binding away from the corner at a 90°angle. Finger press the diagonal fold that forms; then carefully flip binding back onto the quilt top, forming a fold that is parallel to the edge of the quilt. Begin stitching at edge, backstitching to secure.

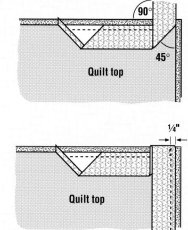

4. Repeat on the remaining three corners. When you reach your starting point, lap the end of the binding over the folded end about 1" and trim away excess binding at a 45° angle. Tuck end into the fold at the beginning of the binding.

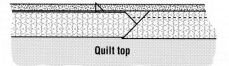

5. Trim away the excess batting and backing, leaving ¼" extending beyond each edge of the quilt. The excess will create a "poof" in the finished binding, making it firm and full. The finished, bound edge will also wear better and longer.

6. Fold binding around batting to the back of the quilt and slipstitch in place along the seam line. A mitered fold will fall into place at each corner. Stitch in place.

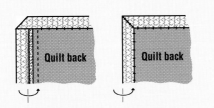

Add a Sleeve and Label

Take the time to make a sleeve for the back of your quilt so it can be hung on the wall. Make a fabric tube almost the width of the finished quilt and hem the ends. Hand stitch the tube to the back of the quilt.

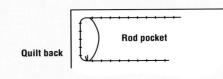

For future generations, be sure to make a label to attach to the back of your quilt. Type, embroider, or cross–stitch on a piece of muslin the name of the quilt, the person who made and quilted it, date completed, owner of quilt, and city and state where it was made. Include any other pertinent information, such as a specific occasion or special fabrics. These labels can be as simple or as fancy as you desire.

Give your beautiful new quilt to a special little someone to love and enjoy!

Quilt Size: 72" x 96"
Block Size: 12"

Materials: 44"-wide fabric

3½ yds. light blue-and-white
  print for background
33 pieces of assorted prints,
  each 9" x 13", for airplanes
¼ yd. plain fabric for
  propellers
1⅔ yds. dark blue print
  for border
6 yds. for backing
1 yd. for binding
76" x 100" piece of batting

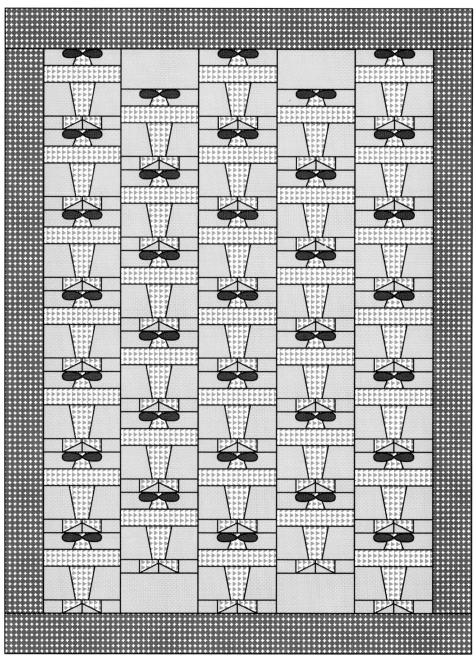

Quilt Plan

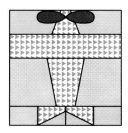

Plane Block
Make 33.

Cutting

Use templates on pages 18–20.

1. From each airplane fabric, cut:
   1 each of Templates A, C, D, and Dr
   1 piece, 3" x 12½", for piece B
2. From paper for paper piecing, cut
   66 Template I.
3. From propeller fabric, cut 66
   Template I, adding ¼" allowance all
   around.
4. Cut the pieces listed in the chart
   below, cutting all strips across the
   fabric width (crosswise grain).

| Fabric | First Cut | | Second Cut | |
	No. of Strips	Strip Width	No. of Pieces	Dimensions
Blocks and Spacers				
Blue-and-white print	2	6½"	4	6½" x 12½" for spacers
	9	5½"	33	Template F
			33r	Template F
	11	3"	33	Template G
			33r	Template G
	6	2½"	66	2½" x 3½" for E
	5	2"	33	Template H
			33r	Template H
Borders				
Dark blue	8	6½"		

Helpful Hint

Here's an easy way to cut those pieces that require reverse pieces.

1. Cut strips of the required width.
2. Fold each strip in half crosswise, with wrong sides together.
3. Position template on the folded strip and cut to yield a pair with one piece reversed.

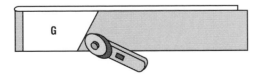

Directions

1. Following the block piecing diagram below, lay out the pieces for each block and sew together in horizontal rows. Press seams toward the airplane pieces.

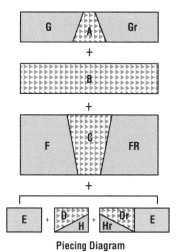

Piecing Diagram

2. Sew rows together to make the block. Make 33 blocks.

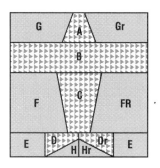

3. Paper piece 66 propellers, following directions for paper piecing on page 11. Appliqué 2 propellers to each block.

4. Referring to the quilt plan on page 16, sew blocks together in vertical rows, adding spacer blocks to the top and bottom edges of rows 2 and 4.

5. Join short ends of border strips to make one long piece; then cut 2 pieces, each 84½" long, for side borders, and 2 pieces, each 72½" long, for top and bottom borders.

6. Sew borders to sides of quilt top and then to the top and bottom edges.

7. Layer the finished quilt top with batting and backing.

8. Pin, baste, quilt, and bind, following the quilt finishing directions that begin on page 12.

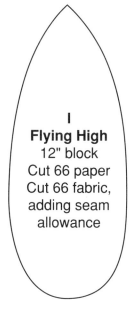

I
Flying High
12" block
Cut 66 paper
Cut 66 fabric,
adding seam
allowance

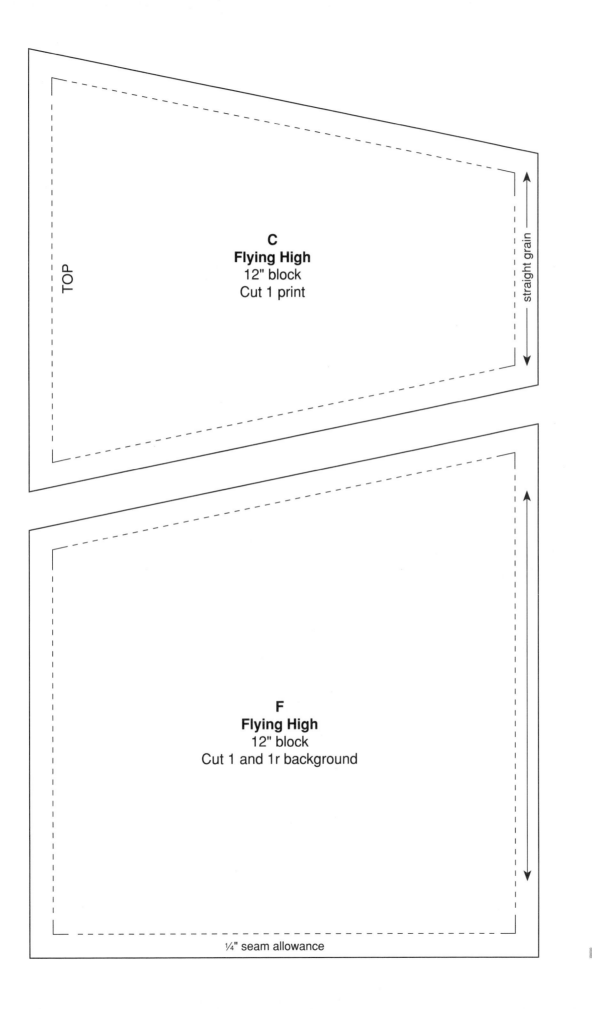

C
Flying High
12" block
Cut 1 print

TOP

straight grain

F
Flying High
12" block
Cut 1 and 1r background

¼" seam allowance

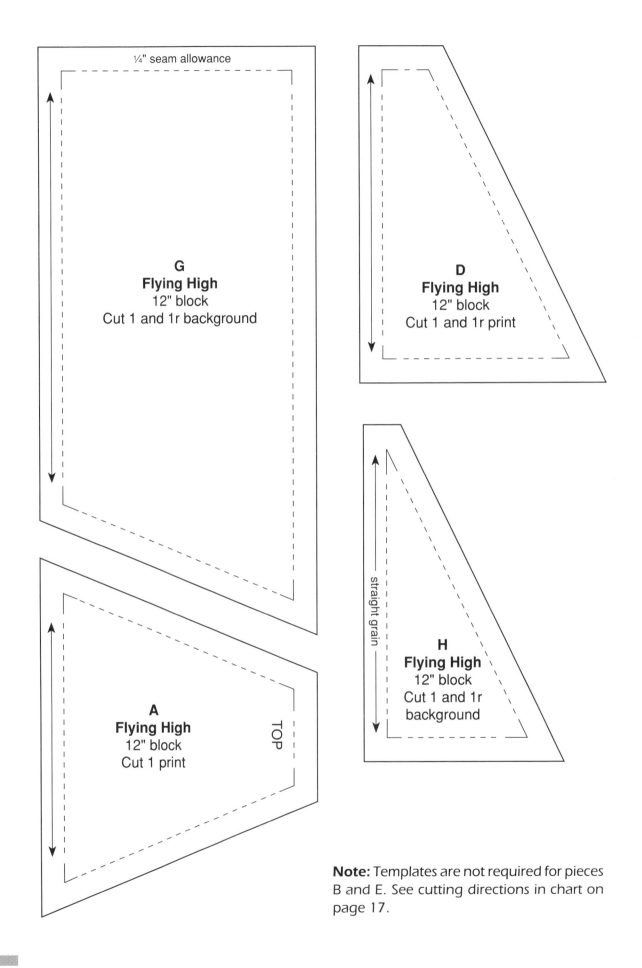

¼" seam allowance

G
Flying High
12" block
Cut 1 and 1r background

D
Flying High
12" block
Cut 1 and 1r print

A
Flying High
12" block
Cut 1 print

TOP

straight grain

H
Flying High
12" block
Cut 1 and 1r
background

Note: Templates are not required for pieces B and E. See cutting directions in chart on page 17.

Wind Spinner

Quilt Plan

Materials: 44"-wide fabric

2½ yds. light print for background (B)

50 pieces assorted prints, each 10" x 14", for pinwheels

50 pieces of solid-colored fabric, each 4¼" square, to coordinate with pinwheel prints*

⅓ yd. black-and-white stripe for stems

⅔ yd. dark blue for borders #1 and #3

¾ yd. print for border #4

4 yds. for backing

⅔ yd. for binding

63" x 82" piece of batting

*From ⅛ yd. solid, you can cut approximately 8 squares.

Pinwheel Block

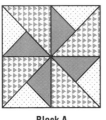

Block A
Make 31.

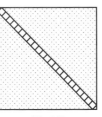

Block B
Make 21.

Block C
Make 7.

Block D
Make 76.

21

Cutting

1. Each Block A has 4 units in identical colors to make the pinwheel. These units are the same as Block D. Following the cutting directions for one pinwheel given below, cut and sew 124 units (31 sets of 4), making sure to use 4 identical units in each block. For border #2, cut and sew a total of 76 Block D (pinwheel) in assorted colors.

    For each pinwheel, cut:
        2 squares, each 3⅞" x 3⅞", then cut once diagonally for 4 triangles

    From matching solid, cut:
        1 square, 4¼" x 4¼"; cut twice diagonally for 4 triangles.
2. Cut the pieces listed in the chart below, cutting all strips across the fabric width (crosswise grain). Some pieces require only one cut, some as many as three.

Fabric	First Cut		Second Cut		Third Cut
	No. of Strips	Strip Width	No. of Pieces	Dimensions	No. of Triangles
All Blocks					
Background	6	4¼"	50	4¼" square	⊠ 200
Block B					
Background	4	7"	23	7" square	◺ 42 for Block B 4 for corner setting triangles
Stripe	6	¾"	21	¾" x 10"	
Block C					
Background	2	6½"	7	6½" square	
Setting Triangles					
Background	2	10"	5	10" square	⊠ 20 for sides
Borders					
Dark blue print	10	1½"			
	3	2"			
	7	3½"			

◺ = Cut once diagonally to yield half-square triangles.

⊠ = Cut twice diagonally to yield quarter-square triangles.

Directions

Block A and Block D

1. Following the block piecing diagram, make 200 pinwheel units.
2. Make 31 Block A, joining 4 units of identical colors for each one. Use the remaining 76 units for Block D.

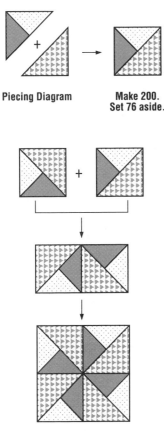

Piecing Diagram

Make 200. Set 76 aside.

Make 31.

Block B

1. Following the piecing diagram, sew 2 background triangles to each stem. Make 21 Block B.
2. Square up blocks to measure 6½".

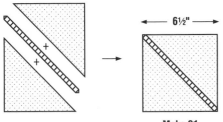

6½"

Make 21.

Quilt Top Assembly and Finishing

1. Following the quilt plan on page 21, sew blocks A, B, and C together in diagonal rows, adding setting triangles as needed.
2. Join rows.
3. Join the short ends of 3 of the 1½"-wide dark blue border strips to make one long strip. Set the remaining 1½"-wide strips aside for the outer border. From the long strip, cut 2 pieces, each 60½" long, for side border #1. Sew to the sides of the quilt top.
4. Join the short ends of the 2"-wide dark blue border strips to make one long strip. Cut 2 pieces, each 45½" long, for top and bottom border #1. Sew to the top and bottom of the quilt top.
5. For pieced border #2, join 21 of Block D together in a vertical row for each side and add to quilt top. For top and bottom borders, join 17 of Block D together in a horizontal row and sew to the top and bottom of the quilt top.
6. Join the short ends of the 7 remaining 1½"-wide border strips to make one long strip. Cut 2 pieces, each 69½" long, for side border #3, and 2 pieces, each 53½" long, for top and bottom border #3. Sew border #3 to the sides and then to the top and bottom of the quilt top.
7. Join the short ends of the 3½"-wide print strips for border #4. Cut 2 pieces, each 71½" long, for side border #4, and 2 pieces, each 59½" long, for top and bottom border #4. Sew to the sides and then to the top and bottom of the quilt top.
8. Layer the finished quilt top with batting and backing.
9. Pin, baste, quilt, and bind, following the quilt finishing directions that begin on page 12.

Quilt Size: 74" x 83"
Block Size: 6" x 12"

Materials: 44"-wide fabric

66 pieces assorted prints, each
    8" x 9", for cats
5 gray fabrics in gradated shades*
    ⅓ yd. #1
    ¾ yd. #2
    1 yd. #3
    ¾ yd. #4
    ⅔ yd. #5
½ yd. red solid for
    inner border
1 yd. red print for
    outer border
5 yds. for backing
1 yd. for binding
78" x 87" piece of batting

*If you prefer a background of
one color, you will need 3½ yds.
of background fabric.

Quilt Plan

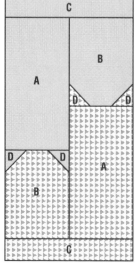

Cat Block
Make 66.

24

Cutting

1. From the assorted red prints for cats, cut the following for each of 66 cats:
   - 1 piece, 3½" x 6½", for A
   - 1 piece, 3½" x 4½", for B
   - 1 piece, 1½" x 6½", for C
   - 2 pieces, each 1½" x 1½", for D
2. Cut the pieces listed in the chart below, cutting all strips across the fabric width (crosswise grain). If using a single background fabric instead of gradated grays, ignore the chart and cut:
   - 21 strips, each 3½" wide. Crosscut 77 pieces, each 3½" x 6½", for 66 piece A and 11 spacer blocks. From the remaining strips, cut 66 pieces, each 3½" x 4½", for B.
   - 16 strips, each 1½" wide. Crosscut 66 pieces, each 1½" x 6½", for C, and132 squares, 1½" x 1½", for D.

Fabric	First Cut		Second Cut	
	No. of Strips	Strip Width	No. of Pieces	Dimensions
Background Cats				
Gray #1	2	3½"	9	3½" x 6½" for A and 3 spacer blocks
			6	3½" x 4½" for B
	2	1½"	6	1½" x 6½" for C
			12	1½" squares for D
Gray #2	5	3½"	16	3½" x 6½" for A and 2 spacer blocks
			14	3½" x 4½" for B
	4	1½"	14	1½" x 6½" for C
			28	1½" squares for D
Gray #3	6	3½"	22	3½" x 6½" for A and 1 spacer block
			21	3½" x 4½" for B
	6	1½"	21	1½" x 6½" for C
			42	1½" squares for D
Gray #4	5	3½"	18	3½" x 6½" for A and 2 spacer blocks
			16	3½" x 4½" for B
	5	1½"	16	1½" x 6½" for C
			32	1½" squares for D

Continued on page 26

Fabric	First Cut		Second Cut	
	No. of Strips	Strip Width	No. of Pieces	Dimensions
Background Cats				
Gray #5	4	3½"	12	3½" x 6½" for A and 3 spacer blocks
			9	3½" x 4½" for B
	3	1½"	9	1½" x 6½" for C
			18	1½" squares for D
Borders				
Red solid	8	1½"		
Red print	8	3½"		

Directions

1. Stack pieces for each cat in separate piles and pin together. Working on the floor or a design wall, place cats in desired arrangement. When satisfied with the layout, add the gray background cats, working from light gray in the upper left corner to dark gray in the lower right corner. (See the quilt photo on page 46.) You will need the following background cats:

   Gray #1 – 6
   Gray #2 – 14
   Gray #3 – 21
   Gray #4 – 16
   Gray #5 – 9

2. Assemble 66 red/gray cat blocks, following the block piecing diagram below and the directions for Quick Geese on page 10.

3. Referring to the quilt plan on page 24 and the color photo on page 48 and taking care to keep each gray in the correct location, arrange the blocks in 11 vertical rows of 6 blocks each. Add spacer blocks to the top or bottom of each row as needed.

4. Sew blocks together in vertical rows; then sew the rows together.

5. Join the short ends of the inner border strips to make one long strip; then cut 2 pieces, each 75½" long, for side borders, and 2 pieces, each 68 ½" long, for top and bottom borders.

6. Join the short ends of the outer border strips to make one long strip; then cut 2 pieces, each 77½" long, for side borders, and 2 pieces, each 74½" long, for top and bottom borders.

7. Sew the inner borders to the sides and then to the top and bottom of the quilt top. Repeat with the outer borders.

8. Layer the finished quilt top with batting and backing.

9. Pin, baste, quilt, and bind, following the quilt finishing directions that begin on page 12.

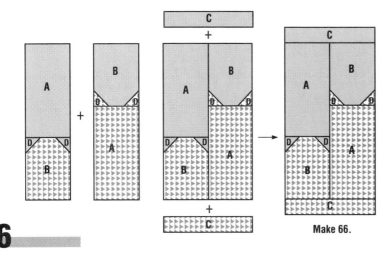

Make 66.

Baby Dream Chaser

Quilt Plan

Materials: 44"-wide fabric

1 yd. background fabric (may be assorted prints in same color or a single fabric)

20 pieces assorted prints, each 8" x 9, for cats

¼ yd. for inner border

1 yd. large print for outer border (may be a single fabric or assorted fabrics for a pieced border like that shown in the quilt photo on page 48)

2 yds. for backing

½ yd. for binding

46" x 67" piece of batting

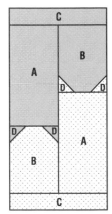

Cutting

1. From the prints for cats, cut the following for each of 20 cats:
   1 piece, 3½" x 6½", for A
   1 piece, 3½" x 4½", for B
   1 piece, 1½" x 6½", for C
   2 pieces, each 1½" x 1½", for D

2. Cut the pieces listed in the chart below, cutting all strips across the fabric width (crosswise grain).

Fabric	First Cut		Second Cut	
	No. of Strips	Strip Width	No. of Pieces	Dimensions
Background Cats and Spacer Blocks				
Background	7	3½"	25	3½" x 6½" for A and 5 spacer blocks
			20	3½" x 4½" for B
	5	1½"	20	1½" x 6½" for C
			40	1½" squares for D
Borders				
Inner border	5	1½"		
Large print	5	5½"		

Directions

1. Stack the pieces for each cat in a separate pile and pin together. Working on the floor or a design wall, place cats in desired arrangement. When satisfied with the layout, add the background cats.
2. Assemble 20 cat blocks, following the block piecing diagram below and the directions for Quick Geese on page 10.
3. Referring to the quilt plan on page 27 and the color photo on page 48, arrange the blocks in 5 vertical rows of 4 blocks each, adding spacer blocks to the top and bottom of the rows as needed.
4. Sew the blocks together in vertical rows; then sew rows together.
5. Join the short ends of the inner border strips to make one long strip. Cut 2 pieces, each 51½" long, for the side borders, and 2 pieces, each 34½" long, for the top and bottom borders. Sew the borders to the sides and then to the top and bottom of the quilt top.
6. Join the short ends of the outer border strips to make one long strip. Cut 2 pieces, each 53½" long, for the side borders, and 2 pieces, each 42½" long, for the top and bottom borders. Sew borders to sides, then to top and bottom of the quilt top.
7. Layer the finished quilt top with batting and backing.
8. Pin, baste, quilt, and bind, following the quilt finishing directions that begin on page 12.

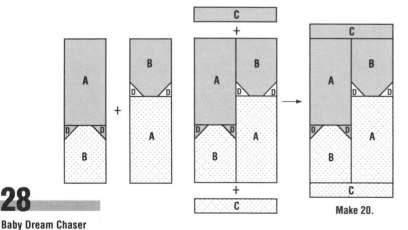

Make 20.

Dancing Snails

Quilt Plan

Materials: 44"-wide fabric
4¼ yds. print for background
1 yd. each of red and blue
    prints
⅔ yd. each of orange, yellow,
    and green prints
5⅓ yds. for backing
1 yd. for binding
76" x 92" piece of batting

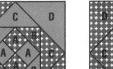

Block 1

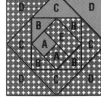

Block 2

Block 3

Block 4

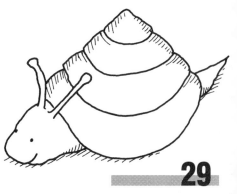

29

Cutting

Cut the pieces* listed in the chart below, cutting all strips across the fabric width (crosswise grain). Some pieces require only one cut, some as many as three.

*When more than one color is listed under "Fabric" in the chart, cut the same number of pieces listed from each fabric.

Fabric	First Cut		Second Cut		Third Cut
	No. of Strips	Strip Width	No. of Pieces	Dimensions	No. of Triangles
Background	4	1⅞"	80	1⅞" square for A	
	5	2⅞"	58	2⅞" square	◻ 116 for B
	5	3⅝"	58	3⅝" square	◻ 116 for C
	8	4⅞"	58	4⅞" square	◻ 116 for D
	1	3¼"	18	1⅞" x 3¼" for E	
	7	8½"	30	8½" square for Block 4	
Red, blue, orange, yellow, and green	1	1⅞"	16	1⅞" square for A	
	1	2⅞"	8	2⅞" square	◻ 16 for B
	1	3⅝"	8	3⅝" square	◻ 16 for C
	1	4⅞"	8	4⅞" square	◻ 16 for D
	1	8½"	4	8½" square for Block 3	

◻ Cut once diagonally to yield half-square triangles.

Directions

1. Arrange all block pieces by size and color.
2. Make Block A, following the piecing diagram.

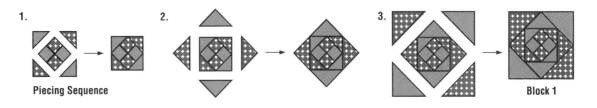

Piecing Sequence · Block 1

Make 3 blocks of each of the following color combinations:

    red/background
    blue/background
    orange/background
    yellow/background
    green/background

Make 4 blocks of each of the following color combinations:

    red/orange/background
    orange/yellow/background
    yellow/green/background
    green/blue/background

Make 3 each.

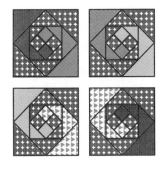

Make 4 each.

3. Make Block B, following the piecing diagram.

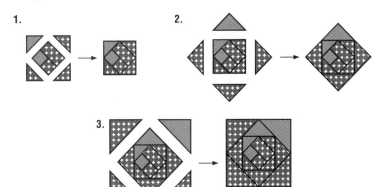

1.

2.

3.

Block 2

Piecing Sequence

Sew 6 blocks of each of the following color combinations:

    red/background
    blue/background

Sew 2 blocks of each of the following color combinations:

    orange/background
    yellow/background
    green/background

Make 2 each.

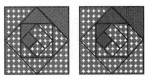

Make 6 each.

4. Following the quilt plan on page 29, arrange the blocks and sew together in horizontal rows. Join the rows to complete the quilt top. Notice that every other row has one solid color. The rows in between share two colors: the color from the row immediately above and the color from the row immediately below, as the snails join hands to dance.

5. Layer the finished quilt top with batting and backing.

6. Pin, baste, quilt, and bind, following the quilt finishing directions that begin on page 12.

Quilt Size: 54" x 65"
Block Size: 8"

Materials: 44"-wide fabric

- 2 yds. pink solid for parasols and inner border
- 2 yds. light pink print for parasol backgrounds
- ⅛ yd. each of 8 assorted pink prints for parasols
- ½ yd. medium pink for the corners of Block B
- ¾ yd. pink print for setting triangles
- ⅔ yd. for outer border
- 2 yds. 22"-wide lightweight sew-in interfacing
- pre-gathered lace or eyelet for embellishment
- 3½ yds. for backing
- ⅔ yd. for binding
- 58" x 69" piece of batting

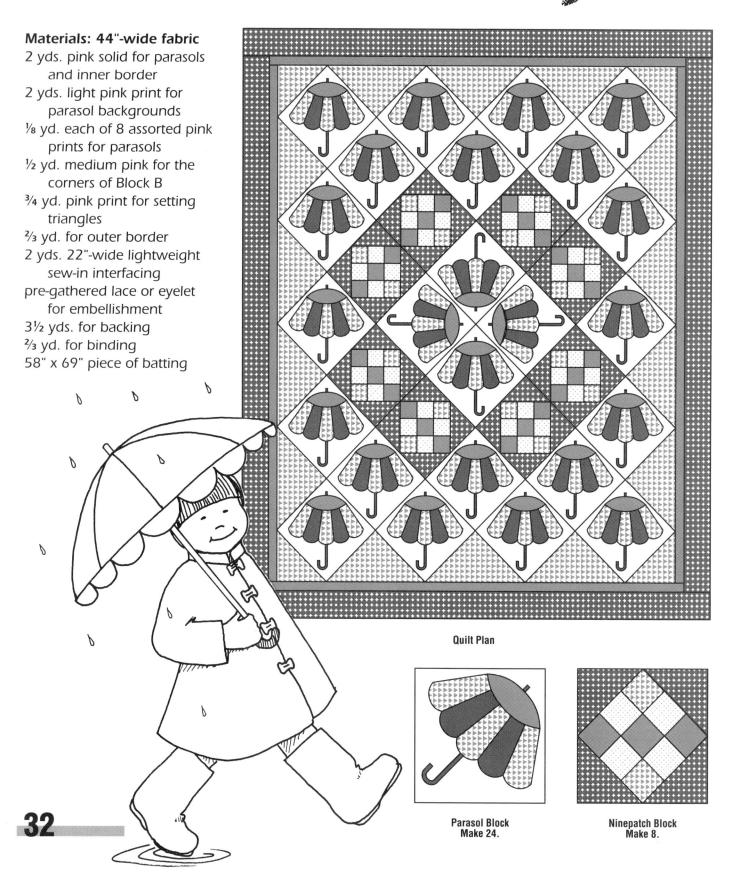

Quilt Plan

Parasol Block
Make 24.

Ninepatch Block
Make 8.

Cutting

Use templates on page 35.

1. From each of the 8 assorted pink prints, cut 9 Template A and 3 Template B for Block A. In addition, cut 2 squares, each 2⅜" x 2⅜", from each print to make Block B.

2. Cut the pieces listed in the chart below, cutting all strips across the fabric width (crosswise grain). Some pieces require only one cut, some as many as three.

Fabric	First Cut No. of Strips	First Cut Strip Width	Second Cut No. of Pieces	Second Cut Dimensions	Third Cut No. of Triangles
Blocks and Borders					
Pink solid	3	4½"	48	Template A	
	3	2⅜"			
	1	5"*			
*See step 1 below for further cutting directions.					
	2	6"	24	Template B	
	6	1½"			
Light pink print	5	8½"	24	8½" square	
	4	2⅜"			
Medium pink print	2	5"	16	5" square	◰ 32 for Block B
Outer border fabric	6	3½"			
Setting Triangles					
Pink print	2	13"	4	13" square	⊠14 (sides)
			2**	8" square	◰ 4 (corners)
** Cut from leftover 13"-wide strip.					

◰ = Cut once diagonally to yield half-square triangles.

⊠ = Cut twice diagonally to yield quarter-square triangles.

Directions

Block A

1. Cut the 5"-wide strip of pink solid into 24 bias strips, each ⅞" wide.
2. Fold each bias strip into thirds lengthwise and press to make 24 strips of bias for handle and parasol tip. Appliqué each handle to a light pink-print background block, following the handle

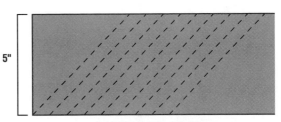

5"

Cut 24 bias strips ⅞" wide.

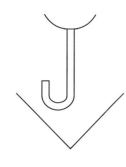

Parasol tip

placement guide on page 35. Fold the leftover from each strip in half for the parasol tip and appliqué in place.

3. Sew 3 pink print Template A and 2 pink solid Template A together, beginning and ending with the prints. Press seams to one side.

4. Sew a Template B to the top edge of each parasol.

5. Interface each parasol. Pin parasol to interfacing, right side down, and cut out interfacing shape. Stitch all the way around the entire piece, using a precise ¼"-wide seam allowance. Trim seam allowance to ⅛" and clip at inner points of scallops. Make a small slit in the interfacing only and then dampen the interfacing so it will be limp.

Interfacing

Slit interfacing.

6. Turn parasol right side out and press. Appliqué to background square, covering the ends of the handle and the parasol tip and inserting lace or eyelet at the bottom edge of the scallops. Make 24 parasol blocks.

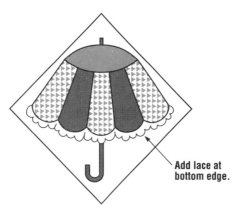

Add lace at bottom edge.

Block B

1. Sew a 2⅜"-wide strip of light pink background print to a 2⅜"-wide strip of pink solid. Crosscut into 16 segments, each 2⅜" wide.

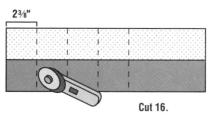

2⅜"

Cut 16.

2. Stitch a pink print square, 2⅜" x 2⅜", to the light square of each segment to make rows 1 and 3 of each Block B.

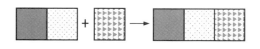

3. Stitch two 2⅜"-wide strips of light pink background print to a pink solid 2⅜"-wide strip as shown. Crosscut 8 segments, each 2⅜" wide, for row 2 of each Block B.

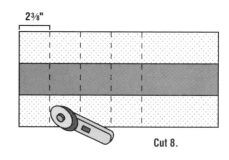

2⅜"

Cut 8.

4. Assemble segments into Ninepatch blocks as shown. Add medium pink print triangles to each side of the completed Ninepatch blocks. Make 8 Ninepatch blocks.

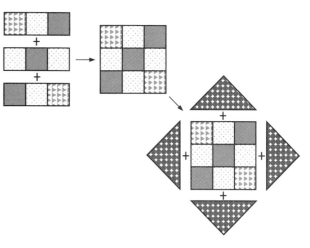

Quilt Top Assembly and Finishing

1. Referring to the quilt plan on page 32, assemble blocks and sew together in diagonal rows, adding setting triangles and corners to beginning and end of each row as needed to complete the quilt top.

2. Join short ends of inner border strips to make one long strip. Cut 2 pieces, each 57½" long, for side borders, and 2 pieces, each 51½" long, for top and bottom borders. Sew borders to the sides and then to the top and bottom of the quilt top.

3. Join the short ends of the outer border strips to make one long strip. Cut 2 pieces, each 59½" long, for side borders, and 2 pieces, each 54½" long, for top and bottom borders. Sew borders to the sides and then to the top and bottom of the quilt top.

4. Layer the finished quilt top with batting and backing.

5. Pin, baste, quilt, and bind, following the quilt finishing directions that begin on page 12.

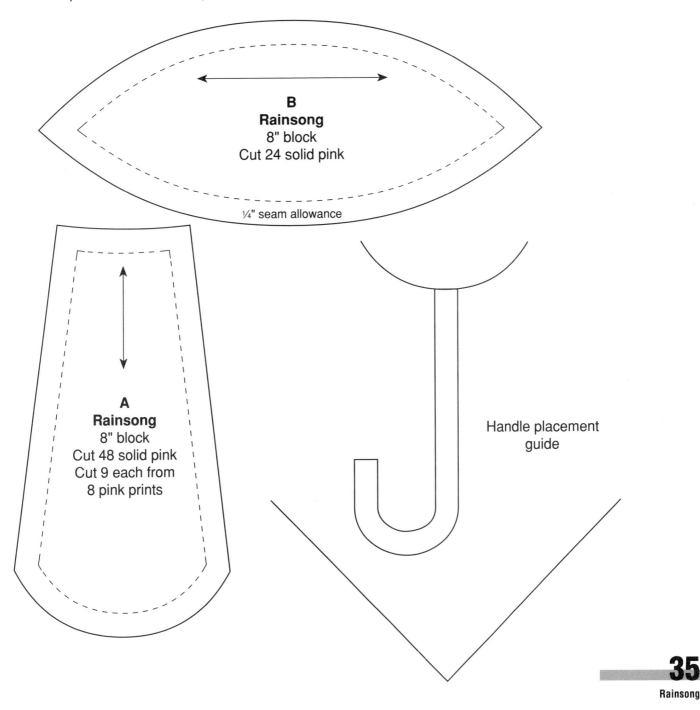

B
Rainsong
8" block
Cut 24 solid pink

¼" seam allowance

A
Rainsong
8" block
Cut 48 solid pink
Cut 9 each from
8 pink prints

Handle placement
guide

Quilt Size: 64" x 76"
Block Size: 8"

Materials: 44"-wide fabric

2¼ yds. blue print for sky
28 pieces, each 6" x 9", in
    assorted bright colors
    for boats and pieced
    border #2
1 yd. white for sails
1 yd. bold print for sashing*
⅔ yd. dark blue for borders
    #1 and #3
1 yd. bold print for
    border #4*
4½ yds. for backing
1 yd. for binding
68" x 80" piece of batting

*If you choose a directional
fabric for the sashing and
outer border, you will need
to adjust the yardage require-
ment and the cutting to take
advantage of the print.

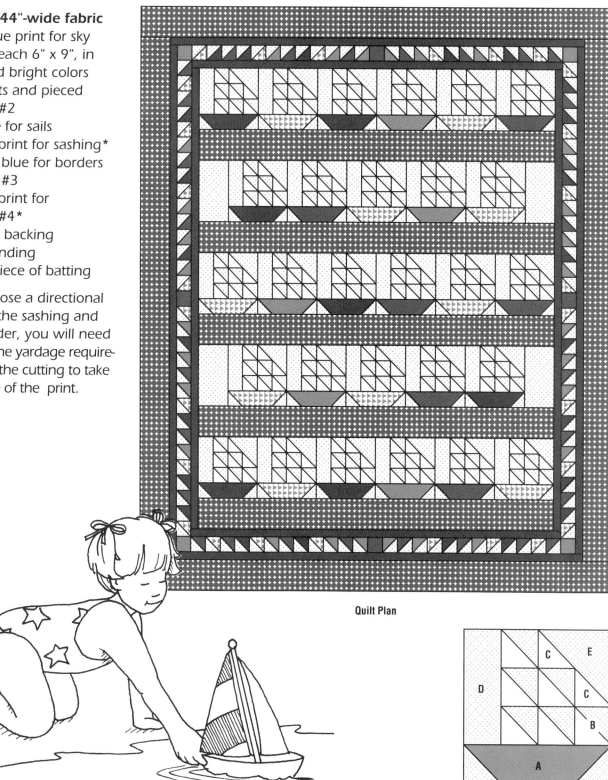

Quilt Plan

Make 28.

Cutting

1. From the assorted boat fabrics, cut 28 pieces, each 2½" x 8½", for A. In addition, cut 8 squares, each 2½" x 2½", for pieced border #2, and 54 squares, each 2⅞" x 2⅞", to pair with sky squares for the pieced border.

2. Cut the pieces listed in the chart below, cutting all strips across the fabric width (crosswise grain). Some pieces require only one cut, some as many as three.

Fabric	First Cut		Second Cut		Third Cut
	No. of Strips	Strip Width	No. of Pieces	Dimensions	No. of Triangles
Blocks					
Blue	9	2½"	56	2½" square	
			28	2½" x 6½" for D	
	2	4⅞"	14	4⅞" square	◻ 28 for E
	11	2⅞"	138	2⅞" square	
	1	4½"	4	4½" x 8½" (spacer blocks)	
White	9	2⅞"	112	2⅞" square	◻ 28* for C
*Set aside remaining 84 squares to pair with sky squares for B.					
Sashing					
Bold print	7	4½"			
Borders #1 and #3					
Dark blue	13	1½"			
Border #4					
Bold print	7	4½"			

◻ = Cut once diagonally to yield half-square triangles.

Directions

1. Following the directions for half-square triangles on page 9, pair and sew 84 sky/sail 2⅞" squares for the blocks, and 54 sky/boat 2⅞" squares for border #2. You will have a total of 168 sky/sail half-square triangle units and 108 sky/boat half-square triangle units. Set the sky/boat units aside for the pieced border.

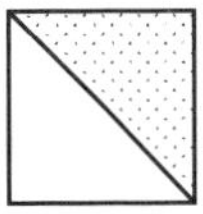

Make 168 Sky/Sail units.

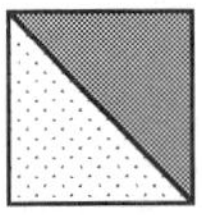

Make 108 Sky/Boat units.

2. Following directions for Quick Geese on page 10, position the 2½" sky squares on each end of the 2½" x 8½" boat segments and sew. Make 28 of these boat units.

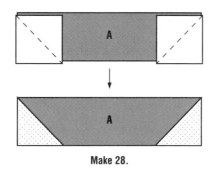

Make 28.

3. Following the diagram below, assemble 28 blocks, using the half-square triangle units, the boat units, and pieces B, C, D, and E.

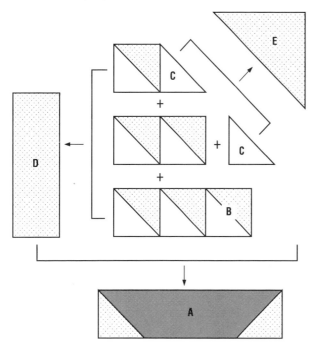

4. Referring to the quilt plan on page 36, arrange the blocks in horizontal rows, adding a spacer block to both ends of row 2 and row 4. Sew blocks and spacers together into rows.

5. Join the short ends of the sashing strips together to make one long strip. Cut 5 pieces, each 48½" long; sew to the bottom of each row. Join rows to complete the quilt top.

6. For border #1, join the short ends of 6 dark blue strips together to make one long strip. Set aside remaining strips for border #3. Cut 2 pieces, each 60½" long, for side borders, and 2 pieces, each 50½" long, for top and bottom borders. Sew border #1 to the sides and then to top and bottom of the quilt top.

7. For each side pieced border #2, join 2 sets of 15 sky/boat units from step 1 to opposite sides of a 2½" boat fabric square, referring to the quilt plan. Sew to the sides of the quilt top. For the top and bottom pieced border, join 2 sets of 12 sky/boat units from step 1 to opposite sides of a 2½" boat fabric square. Add a 2½" square at each end of the top and bottom pieced borders. Sew pieced borders to the top and bottom edges of the quilt top.

8. For border #3, join the short ends of the remaining 7 dark blue border strips together to make one long strip. Cut 2 pieces, each 68½" long, for the side borders, and 2 pieces, each 56½" long, for the top and bottom borders. Sew border #3 to the sides and then to the top and bottom of the quilt top.

9. Join the short ends of the strips for border #4 together to make one long strip. Cut 2 pieces, each 68 ½" long, for the side borders, and 2 pieces, each 64 ½" long, for the top and bottom borders. Sew border #4 to the sides and then to the top and bottom of the quilt top.

10. Layer the finished quilt top with batting and backing.

11. Pin, baste, quilt, and bind, following the quilt finishing directions that begin on page 12.

Baby Windsails

Quilt Plan

Materials: 44"-wide fabric
1¼ yds. blue for sky
14 pieces, each 3" x 9", in assorted bright colors for boats
½ yd. white for sails
½ yd. bold print for sashing
⅓ yd. red for inner border
½ yd. bold print for outer border
1⅔ yds. backing
⅔ yd. red for binding
44" x 56" piece of batting

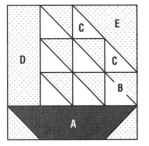

Make 14.

Cutting

1. From the assorted boat fabrics, cut 14 pieces, each 2½" x 8½", for A.
2. Cut the pieces listed in the chart below, cutting all strips across the fabric width (crosswise grain). Some pieces require only one cut, some as many as three.

Fabric	First Cut		Second Cut		Third Cut
	No. of Strips	Strip Width	No. of Pieces	Dimensions	No. of Triangles
Blocks					
Blue	5	2½"	28	2½" square	
			14	2½" x 6½" for D	
	1	4⅞"	7	4⅞" square	◿ 14 for E
	6	2⅞"	42	2⅞" square	
	1	4½"	4	4½" x 8½" (spacer blocks)	
White	5	2⅞"	56	2⅞" square	◿ 14* for C
	*Set aside remaining 42 to pair with sky squares for B.				
Sashing					
Bold print	4	3½"			
Borders					
Red	4	1½"			
Bold print	5	3½"			
◿ = Cut once diagonally to yield half-square triangles.					

Directions

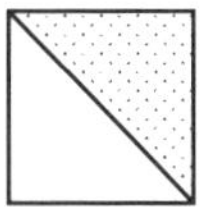

Make 84 Sky/Sail units.

1. Following the directions for half-square triangles on page 9, pair and sew 42 sky/sail 2⅞" squares for the blocks. You will have 84 half–square triangle units after stitching and cutting.

2. Follow steps 2 and 3 for the larger Windsails quilt on page 38.

3. Referring to the quilt plan on page 39, arrange boat blocks in horizontal rows, adding spacer blocks to both ends of row 2 and row 4. Sew together into rows.

4. Join the short ends of the sashing strips together to make one long strip. Cut 4 pieces, each 32½" long; sew to the bottom of each row of blocks. Sew rows together to complete quilt top.

5. Join the short ends of the inner border strips together to make one long strip. Cut 2 pieces, each 44½" long, for the side borders, and 2 pieces, each 34½" long, for the top and bottom borders. Sew the inner borders to the sides and then to the top and bottom of the quilt top.

6. Join the short ends of the outer border strips together to make one long strip. Cut 2 pieces, each 46½" long, for the side borders, and 2 pieces, each 40½" long, for the top and bottom borders. Sew the outer borders to the sides and then to top and bottom of the quilt top.

7. Layer the finished quilt top with batting and backing.

8. Pin, baste, quilt, and bind, following the quilt finishing directions that begin on page 12.

(Above left) **Wind Spinner,** made and quilted by Carolann M. Palmer, 1992, Seattle, Washington, 59" x 78". Pinwheels on striped stems whirl colorfully in the summer breeze.

(Above right) **Flower Garden,** made by Judy Pollard, 1993, Seattle, Washington, 59" x 78". Judy added appliquéd leaves to Carolann's original Wind Spinner design to create this quilt garden of happy flowers. Quilted by Virginia Lauth.

(Left) **Dancing Snails,** made and quilted by Carolann M. Palmer, 1992, Seattle, Washington, 72" x 88". These colorful creatures tango their way across the quilt surface in the popular Snails Trail pattern.

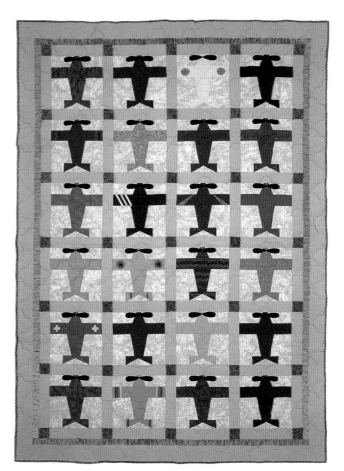

(Below) **Lift Anchor,** made and quilted by Carolann M. Palmer, 1992, Seattle, Washington, 66" x 80". This red, white, and blue version of a Brooks/Wheeler design would inspire the most reluctant landlubber to take to the high seas.

(Right) **Bill's Squadron,** made by Arlene Sheckler, 1993, Bothell, Washington, 72" x 100". Taking off to dreamland, this spectacular air show of flying aces transports its young owner across a quilted sky. Note the novel embellishments on each plane in this Flying High variation. Quilted by Sue Lohse.

(Below Right) **Flying High,** made and quilted by Carolann M. Palmer, 1991, Seattle, Washington, 72" x 96". The vertical setting for this old Aunt Martha pattern puts the scrappy planes in flying formation. Bright patterns streak across a quilted sky. Happy landing!

(Above left) **Hitch Your Sailboat to a Star,** made and quilted by Deann Thompson, 1993, Seattle, Washington, 40" x 52". With stars to guide them, these ships set sail for dreamland across a crib-sized quilted sea. Owned by Benjamin Thompson.

(Above) **Windsails,** made and quilted by Carolann M. Palmer, 1992, Seattle, Washington, 64" x 76". A fanciful regatta sails across the sea. Underwater, colorful fish swim gracefully beneath the brightly colored hulls.

(Left) **Baby Windsails,** made and quilted by Carolann M. Palmer, 1992, Seattle, Washington, 40" x 52". Owned by Timothy Hammer. Balmy breezes blow and tropical fish swim, setting a perfect scene for sailing the seas.

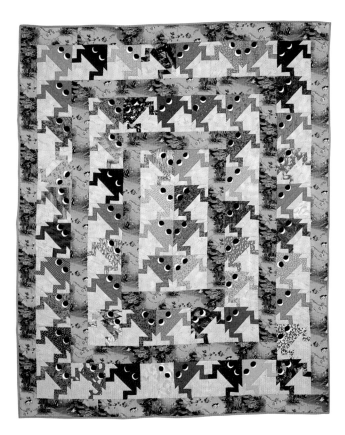

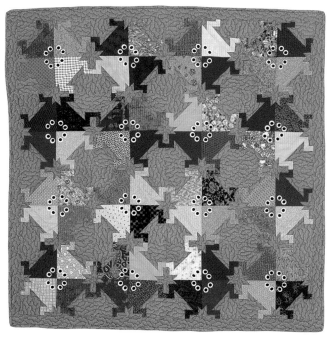

(Above left) **Frog Pond,** made and quilted by Carolann M. Palmer, 1992, Seattle, Washington, 72" x 88". Amphibians in formation are the basis of this eye-popping, frog-hopping, pieced pond of a quilt.

(Above right) **Synchronized Swimming,** made and quilted by Bev Bodine, 1993, Mountlake Terrace, Washington, 62" x 62". Olympic form and style are sure to capture a gold medal for these athletic amphibians.

(Right) **Bird Garden,** made and quilted by Carolann M. Palmer, 1992, Seattle, Washington, 59" x 74". Many varieties of appliquéd birds nest in a garden sashed with flowered strips.

(Above left) **Dream Wardrobe—Boy,** made and quilted by Carolann M. Palmer, 1992, Seattle, Washington, 42" x 54". Shirts and pants pieced from scraps illustrate a modern boy's wardrobe choices.

(Above right) **Dream Wardrobe,** made and quilted by Nancy Ewell, 1993, Seattle, Washington, 42" x 54", for granddaughter Theresa Ewell. Lace and ribbon adorn paper-doll-like dresses.

(Left) **Dream Wardrobe—Girl,** made and quilted by Carolann M. Palmer, 1992, Seattle, Washington, 67" x 76". This is a special memory quilt, lovingly compiled from scraps of real dresses. Perfect embellishments of buttons, ribbons, and lace "dress up" these fanciful frocks.

(Above left) **Rainsong,** made and quilted by Carolann M. Palmer, 1992, Seattle, Washington, 54" x 65". Rain makes a pretty sound when falling on these eyelet-trimmed umbrellas.

(Above right) **Baby Fanfleur,** made and quilted by Carolann M. Palmer, 1992, Seattle, Washington, 40" x 56". A bright garden of flowers and butterflies in a crib-sized quilt brings warmth to the nursery.

(Right) **Fanfleur,** made and quilted by Carolann M. Palmer, 1992, Seattle, Washington, 72" x 72". Summer garden colors and easy machine-appliquéd flowers and butterflies combine to create this happy quilt.

(Left) **Crown Jewels,** made and quilted by Carolann M. Palmer, 1992, Seattle, Washington, 60" x 76". Carolann's choice of a primary-colored "junk food" print adds whimsy to this quilt in an easy pattern to cut and piece.

(Below left) **Baby Crown Jewels,** made and quilted by Carolann M. Palmer, 1992, Seattle, Washington, 44" x 60". Theme fabrics of fire engines and Dalmatian spots (on back of quilt) combine to fascinate the smallest firefighter.

(Below right) **Veronica's World,** made and quilted by Martha Ahern, 1993, Everett, Washington, 52" x 52", for granddaughter Veronica Coburn. The imaginative use of theme fabrics in this simple Crown Jewels design features some of earth's precious jewels.

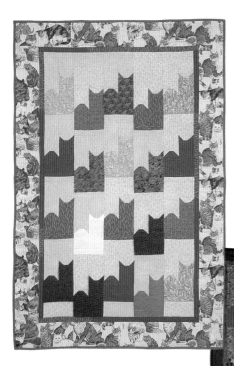

(Above) **Baby Dream Chaser,** made and quilted by Carolann M. Palmer, 1992, Seattle, Washington, 42" x 63". This crib-sized quilt features tessellated litters of kittens dreaming of their own playful chases.

(Above right) **Dream Chaser,** made and quilted by Carolann M. Palmer, 1992, Seattle, Washington, 74" x 83". Napping cats, dreaming of a chase, repose on this quilt. When viewed upside down, the tessellated design reveals just as many gray cats joining in the dream!

(Middle) **My Jungle Cats,** made by Marjorie Meyers, 1993, Bothell, Washington, 74" x 83". Wild animal prints tame the "big" cats in a tessellated jungle. Quilted by Maggie Kamikawa.

(Right) **Alex Cats**, made and quilted by Joyce S. Miller, 1993, Edmonds, Washington, 74" x 83". These calico felines no doubt dream of chasing the "China dog" with their tessellated shadows. Alex Ebersole is the proud owner of this group of unique alley cats.

Lift Anchor

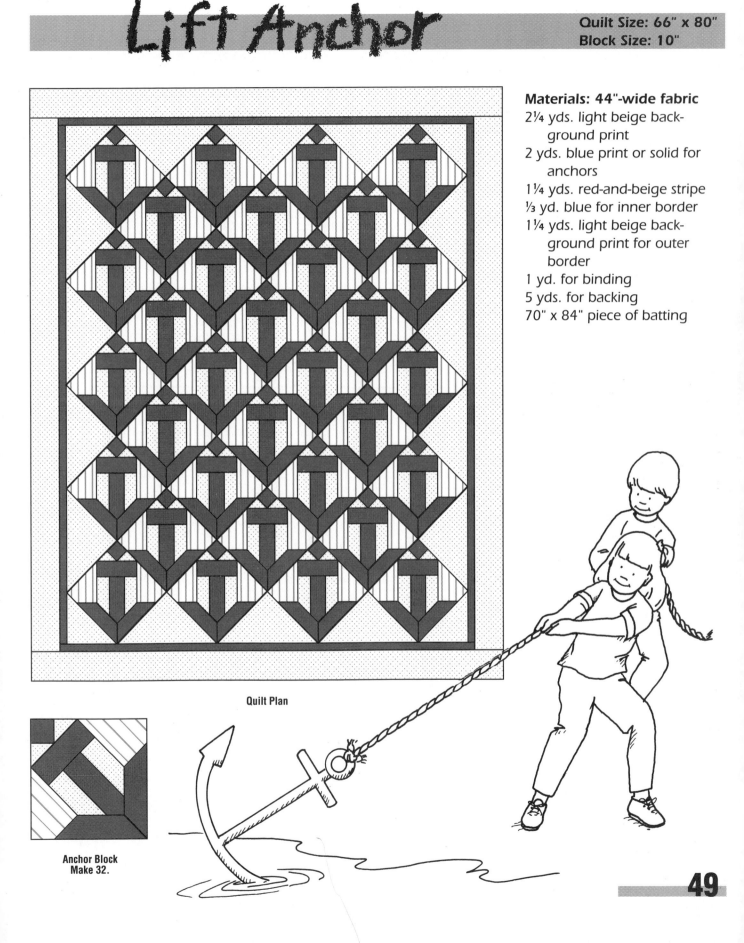

Quilt Plan

**Anchor Block
Make 32.**

Materials: 44"-wide fabric
2¼ yds. light beige background print
2 yds. blue print or solid for anchors
1¼ yds. red-and-beige stripe
⅓ yd. blue for inner border
1¼ yds. light beige background print for outer border
1 yd. for binding
5 yds. for backing
70" x 84" piece of batting

Cutting

Use templates on pages 51–52.

Cut the pieces listed in the chart below, cutting all strips across the fabric width (crosswise grain). Some pieces require only one cut, some as many as three.

Fabric	First Cut		Second Cut		Third Cut
	No. of Strips	Strip Width	No. of Pieces	Dimensions	No. of Triangles
Blocks					
Light beige print	9	2¼"	32	Template F	
			32	Template Fr	
	3	2⅞"	32	2⅞" square	◿ 64 for G
Blue	14	2½"	64	Template A	
			32	2½" square for D	
	12	2⅝"	32	Template B	
			32	2⅝" x 6⅛" for C	
Stripe	6	6½"	32	Template E	
			32	Template Er	
Setting Triangles					
Background	2	16"	4	16" square	⊠14 for sides
	1	8"	2	8" square	◿4 for corners
Borders					
Blue	7	1½"			
Light beige print	8	4½"			

◿ = Cut once diagonally to yield half-square triangles.

⊠ = Cut twice diagonally to yield quarter-square triangles.

Directions

1. Assemble the upper unit of each block as shown below.

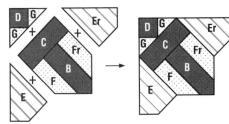
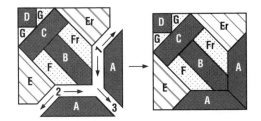

2. Attach the bottom of the anchor (A) to each side of the block, following the direction of the arrows.

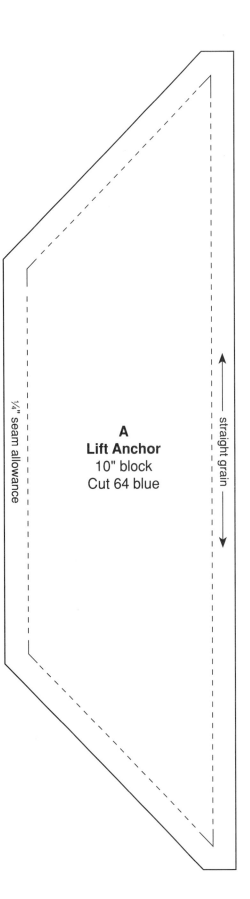

   Stitch the seam at the point of the anchor last.

3. Referring to the quilt plan on page 49, arrange blocks and side and corner setting triangles. Sew blocks and setting triangles together in diagonal rows. Join the rows, adding the side and corner triangles.

4. Join the short ends of the inner border strips to make one long strip. Cut 2 pieces, each 71½" long, for the side borders, and 2 pieces, each 58½" long, for the top and bottom borders. Sew inner borders to the sides and then to the top and bottom of the quilt top.

5. Join the short ends of the outer border strips to make one long strip. Cut 2 pieces, each 73½" long, for the side borders, and 2 pieces, each 66½" long, for the top and bottom borders. Sew outer borders to the sides and then to the top and bottom of the quilt top.

6. Layer the finished quilt top with batting and backing.

7. Pin, baste, quilt, and bind, following the quilt finishing directions on page 12.

¼" seam allowance

straight grain

A
Lift Anchor
10" block
Cut 64 blue

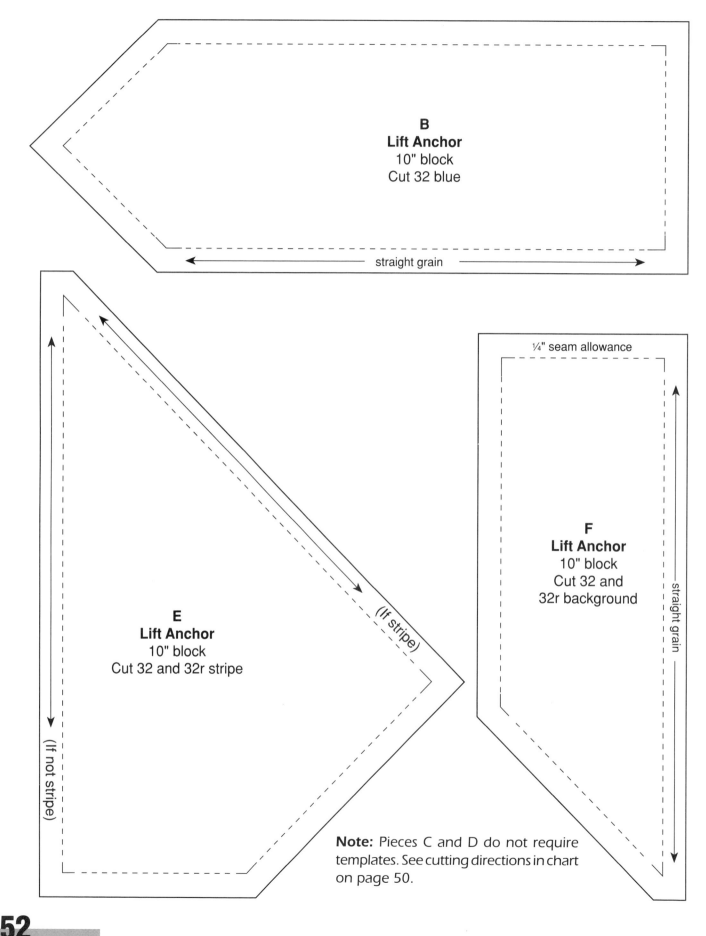

B
Lift Anchor
10" block
Cut 32 blue

← straight grain →

¼" seam allowance

F
Lift Anchor
10" block
Cut 32 and
32r background

straight grain

(If stripe)

E
Lift Anchor
10" block
Cut 32 and 32r stripe

(If not stripe)

Note: Pieces C and D do not require templates. See cutting directions in chart on page 50.

Fanfleur

Quilt Size: 72" x 72"
Block Size: 8"

Quilt Plan

Fan Block

Materials: 44"-wide fabric

3¼ yds. light print or solid for background
⅔ yd. purple #1 for flower petals
⅔ yd. purple #2 for alternate flower petals
¼ yd. purple solid for flower centers
¼ yd. blue #1 for half-flower petals
¼ yd. blue #2 for alternate half-flower petals
¼ yd. blue solid for half-flower centers
⅔ yd. pink #1 for butterflies
½ yd. pink #2 for alternate butterfly wings
¼ yd. pink solid for butterfly centers
⅔ yd. purple #3 for butterflies
½ yd. purple #4 for alternate butterfly wings
¼ yd. purple solid for butterfly centers
6 yds. 22"-wide sew-in interfacing
⅓ yd. purple for inner border
¾ yd. print for outer border
5 yds. for backing
1 yd. for binding
1 skein black embroidery floss for butterfly antennae

53

Cutting

Use templates on page 56.

Cut the pieces listed in the chart below, cutting all strips across the fabric width (crosswise grain).

Fabric	First Cut		Second Cut	
	No. of Strips	Strip Width	No. of Pieces	Dimensions
All Blocks				
Light background	13	8½"	64	8½" square
Flower Blocks				
Purple #1	3	6½"	50	Template A
Purple #2	3	6½"	50	Template A
Purple solid	2	3"	20	Template B
Blue #1	1	6½"	20	Template A
Blue #2	1	6½"	20	Template A
Blue solid	1	3"	8	Template B
Butterfly Blocks				
Pink #1	3	6½"	48	Template A
Pink #2	2	6½"	32	Template A
Pink solid	1	3"	16	Template B
Purple #3	3	6½"	48	Template A
Purple #4	2	6½"	32	Template A
Purple solid	1	3"	16	Template B
Borders				
Purple	7	1½"		
Print	7	3½"		

Directions

Butterfly Blocks

1. For butterflies, make 16 pink and 16 purple Fan blocks. Beginning and ending with print #1, alternate piece A in prints #1 and #2 to make a 5-piece fan unit. Press seams to one side.

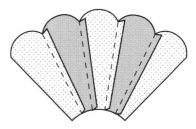

2. Place fan right side down on a piece of lightweight interfacing. Pin in place, then cut a fan shape from the interfacing, using the fan as a pattern. Stitch around the curved edge, using a precise ¼"-wide seam allowance. Trim seam to ⅛" and clip at inner corners.

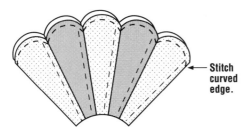

Stitch curved edge.

3. Spray interfacing with water, so it goes limp for ease in turning. Turn and press. Appliqué each completed fan to one corner of a background square.

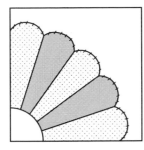

4. Cut a piece of interfacing for each piece B and stitch to the curved edge. Trim seam, dampen as described above, turn, and press. Appliqué the curved edge to the fan, folding the background square out of the way so you don't catch it in the stitches. Press.

5. Square up edges to match edges of background square if necessary. Then, cut away the background square behind the fan and fan center, leaving a ¼" allowance all around.

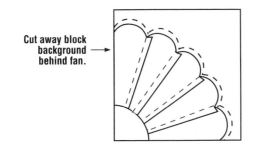

Cut away block background behind fan.

Flower Blocks

1. Make the flower blocks, following the directions for the Butterfly blocks. Use the blocks below as color placement guides to make 10 each of Flower A and B blocks in purple and 4 each in blue.

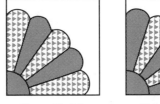
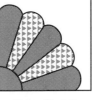

Flower Block A
Make 10 purple.
Make 4 blue.

Flower Block B
Make 10 purple.
Make 4 blue.

2. Add flower centers (Template B) in matching solid color.

3. Using the antennae placement guide on page 56 and referring to the quilt plan on page 53, embroider antennae in one corner of:
    - 4 light background corner blocks
    - 8 blue Flower blocks
    - 2 purple Flower A blocks
    - 2 purple Flower B blocks

Quilt Top Assembly and Finishing

1. Referring to the quilt plan on page 53, arrange blocks to form flowers and butterflies, adding the 4 remaining background blocks in the corners.

2. Sew blocks together into horizontal rows; then sew rows together.

3. Join the short ends of the inner border strips to make one long strip. Cut 2 pieces, each 64½" long, for the side borders, and 2 pieces, each 66½" long, for the top and bottom borders. Sew the inner borders to the sides and then to the top and bottom of the quilt top.

4. Join the short ends of the outer border strips to make one long strip. Cut 2 pieces, each 66½" long, for the side borders, and 2 pieces, each 72½" long, for the top and bottom borders. Sew the outer borders to the sides and then to the top and bottom of the quilt top.

5. Layer the finished quilt top with batting and backing.

6. Pin, baste, quilt, and bind, following the quilt finishing directions that begin on page 12.

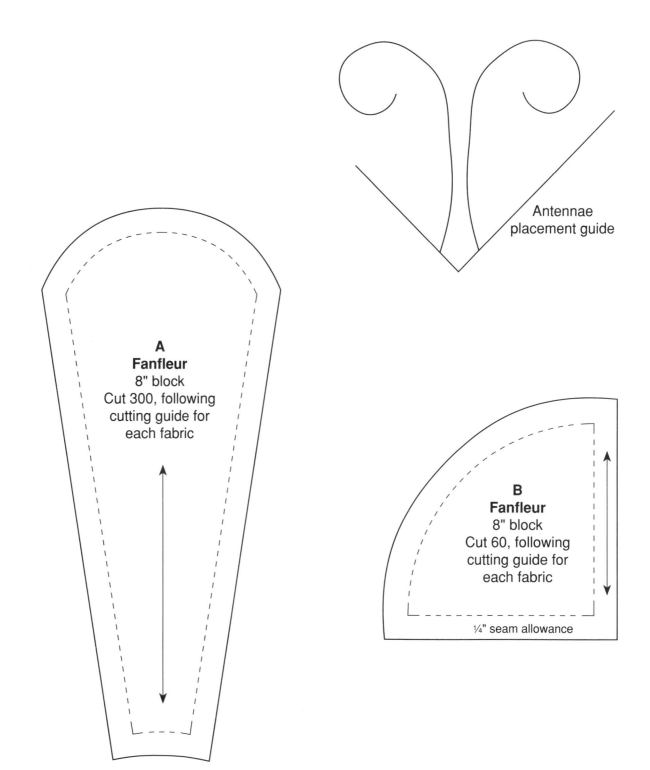

Antennae
placement guide

A
Fanfleur
8" block
Cut 300, following
cutting guide for
each fabric

B
Fanfleur
8" block
Cut 60, following
cutting guide for
each fabric

¼" seam allowance

Baby Fanfleur

Materials: 44"-wide fabric

- 2 yds. light background print or solid
- ¼ yd. orange #1 for flower petals
- ¼ yd. orange #2 for alternate flower petals
- ⅛ yd. orange solid for flower centers
- ½ yd. turquoise #1 for butterflies and corner flowers
- ⅔ yd. turquoise #2 for alternate butterfly wings and corner flowers
- ⅛ yd. turquoise solid for butterfly and flower centers
- 2 yds. 22"-wide sew-in interfacing
- ¼ yd. orange for inner border
- ⅔ yd. turquoise print for outer border
- 2 yds. for backing
- ⅔ yd. for binding
- 1 skein black embroidery floss for butterfly antennae
- 44" x 60" piece of batting

Quilt Plan

Fan Block

Cutting

Use templates on page 56.

Cut the pieces listed in the chart below, cutting all strips across the fabric width (crosswise grain).

Fabric	First Cut No. of Strips	First Cut Strip Width	Second Cut No. of Pieces	Second Cut Dimensions
Blocks				
Background	7	8½"	24	8½" square
Orange #1	1	6½"	20	Template A
Orange #2	1	6½"	20	Template A
Orange solid	1	3"	8	Template B
Turquoise #1	2	6½"	36	Template A
Turquoise #2	3	6½"	44	Template A
Turquoise solid	1	3"	16	Template B
Borders				
Orange	5	1½"		
Turquoise print	5	3½"		

Flower Block A
Make 4 orange.

Flower Block B
Make 4 orange.

Flower Block B
Make 4 turquoise.

Butterfly Block A
Make 4 turquoise.

Butterfly Block B
Make 8 turquoise.

Directions

1. Make the Butterfly and Flower blocks, following the directions for the larger Fanfleur quilt on pages 53–56. Make 4 each of Flower Blocks A and B in orange. Make 4 of Flower Block B in turquoise. Make 4 Butterfly Block A and 8 Butterfly Block B in turquoise.

2. Using the antennae placement guide on page 56, embroider antennae in one corner of:
   2 orange Flower Block A
   2 orange Flower Block B

3. Referring to the quilt plan on page 57, arrange blocks to form flowers and butterflies.

4. Sew blocks together into horizontal rows; then sew rows together.

5. Join the short ends of the inner border strips to make one long strip. Cut 2 pieces, each 48½" long, for side borders, and 2 pieces, each 34½" long, for top and bottom borders. Sew the inner borders to the sides and then to the top and bottom of the quilt top.

6. Join the short ends of the outer border strips to make one long strip. Cut 2 pieces, each 50½" long, for the side borders and 2 pieces, each 40½" long, for the top and bottom borders. Sew the outer borders to the sides and then to the top and bottom of the quilt top.

7. Layer the finished quilt top with batting and backing.

8. Pin, baste, quilt, and bind, following the quilt finishing directions that begin on page 12.

Bird Garden

Materials: 44"-wide fabric

1½ yds. light print for block backgrounds

½ yd. print for nests*

24 assorted prints, each 7" x 7", for birds

⅓ yd. print for wings*

⅛ yd. for bird beaks

2 yds. for setting triangles (sides and corners)

2 yds. of a striped print with striped designs that are 3" wide, finished, for borders and sashing**

4 yds. for backing

1 yd. for binding

63" x 78" piece of batting

* You may use assorted scraps totaling this amount if you prefer.

** You will need to be able to cut 8 lengths of the stripe in the chosen print. If this is not possible in your chosen fabric, you will need 14 running yards of a 3½"-wide stripe (3" finished).

**Bird Block
Make 24.**

Quilt Plan

Cutting

Use templates on page 62.

Cut the pieces listed in the chart below, cutting all strips across the fabric width (crosswise grain). Some pieces require only two cuts, some as many as three. Cutting for birds, borders, and sashing strips are included within the assembly directions.

Fabric	First Cut		Second Cut		Third Cut
	No. of Strips	Strip Width	No. of Pieces	Dimensions	No. of Triangles
Blocks					
Background	5	8½"	24	8½" square	
Nest print	5	2⅝"	24	9¾" trapezoids*	
*See page 9 for cutting trapezoids from strips.					
Beak fabric	2	1½"	24	1½" square	
Setting Triangles					
Print	4	12½"	10	12½" square	⊠ 40 for sides
	2	6⅝"	8	6⅝" square	◻ 16 for corners

◻ = Cut once diagonally to yield half-square triangles.

⊠ = Cut twice diagonally to yield quarter-square triangles.

Directions

1. To prepare the background blocks, measure out and mark a point 6³⁄₁₆" from the corner on 2 adjacent sides. Position ruler at these 2 points and cut away the corner triangle as shown. Set aside the larger piece for the top corner of the block.

2. From the long edge of the triangle, cut a strip 1⅝" wide. Discard. Use the remaining small triangle for the bottom corner of each bird block.

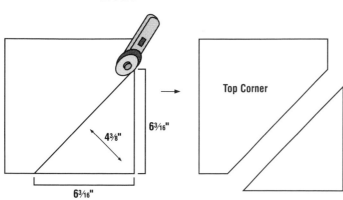

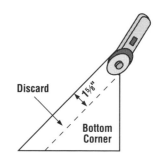

3. Assemble the pieced background blocks as shown.

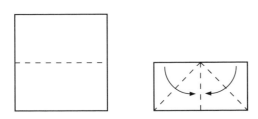

4. To prepare the beak for each block, fold each beak square in half; then bring folded edge to the center as shown.

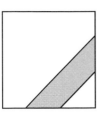

5. Using Templates A and B, cut 24 bird bodies and 24 wings from freezer paper. Cut 24 birds and 24 wings from the assorted fabrics, adding ¼" allowance all around each piece. Prepare for paper-pieced appliqué as shown on page 11.

6. Appliqué the bird body to the pieced block, aligning the bottom edge of the body with the nest, and inserting beak. Add the wing.

Make 24.

7. Embroider an eye on each bird or add with a fabric marker.

8. For sashing and borders, cut enough 3½"-wide strips to total 14 yards, cutting along the fabric length. Join the short ends of the strips to make one long piece. From the strip, cut:
   3 pieces, each 3½" x 68½", for vertical sashings
   2 pieces, each 3½" x 76", for side borders
   2 pieces, each 3½" x 62", for top and bottom borders

9. Arrange the blocks and side and corner triangles into 4 vertical rows of 6 blocks each as shown at right. Sew the pieces together in each row on the diagonal.

10. Join the rows with vertical sashing strips.

11. Sew the borders to the sides and then to the top and bottom of the quilt top, mitering corners if desired.

12. Layer the finished quilt top with batting and backing.

13. Pin, baste, quilt, and bind, following the quilt finishing directions that begin on page 12.

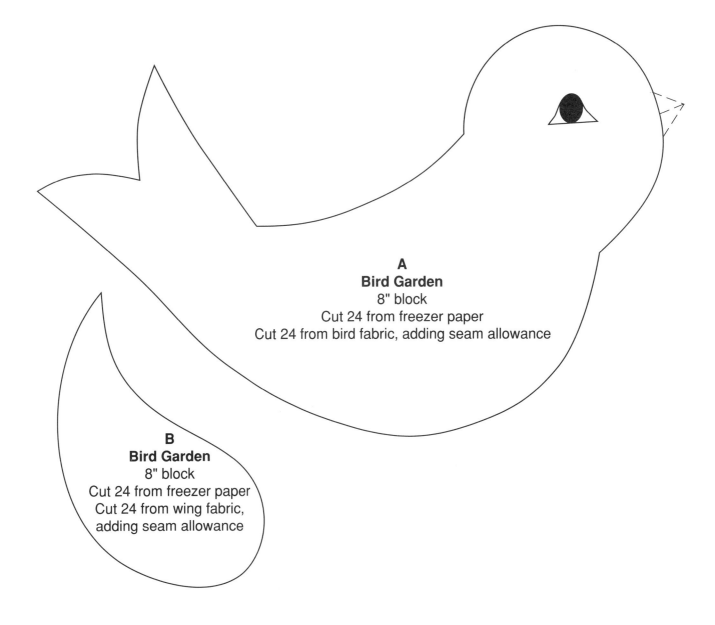

A
Bird Garden
8" block
Cut 24 from freezer paper
Cut 24 from bird fabric, adding seam allowance

B
Bird Garden
8" block
Cut 24 from freezer paper
Cut 24 from wing fabric,
adding seam allowance

Crown Jewels

Materials: 44"-wide fabric

1⅓ yds. light print for background

1 yd. dark blue print

¼ yd. green print or solid

1 yd. red print

¼ yd. yellow print or solid

1 yd. yellow print or solid for inner border

1 yd. dark blue print for outer border

4 yds. for backing

⅔ yd. dark blue solid for binding

64" x 80" piece of batting

Quilt Plan

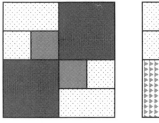

Block A

Block B

Cutting

Cut the pieces listed in the chart below, cutting all strips across the fabric width (crosswise grain).

Fabric	First Cut		Second Cut	
	No. of Strips	Strip Width	No. of Pieces	Dimensions
Blocks				
Light print	18*	2½"	96	2½" x 4½"
	*Set aside 6 strips for strip piecing, step 1 below.			
Dark blue	6	4½"	48	4½" square
Green	3	2½"		
Red	6	4½"	48	4½" square
Yellow	3	2½"		
Borders				
Yellow	7	2½"		
Dark blue	7	4½"		

Directions

1. Strip piece 3 units composed of 2½"-wide light background and green strips. Crosscut 48 pieces, each 2½" wide. Repeat with the remaining light background strips and the yellow strips.

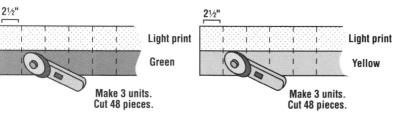

2. Assemble the blocks, following the piecing diagram below. Use dark blue and red squares, background rectangles, and the units made in step 1.

3. Referring to the quilt plan on page 63, arrange the blocks into horizontal rows. Sew together in rows; then sew rows together.

4. Join the short ends of the yellow inner border strips to make one long strip. Cut 2 pieces, each 64½" long, for the side borders, and 2 pieces, each 52½" long, for the top and bottom borders. Sew the inner borders to the sides and then to the top and bottom of the quilt top.

5. Join the short ends of the dark blue outer border strips to make one long strip. Cut 2 pieces, each 68½" long, for the side borders and 2 pieces, each 60½" long, for the top and bottom borders. Sew the outer borders to the sides and then to the top and bottom of the quilt top.

6. Layer the finished quilt top with batting and backing.

7. Pin, baste, quilt, and bind, following the quilt finishing directions that begin on page 12.

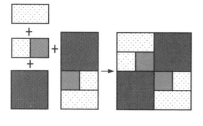

Block A
Make 24.

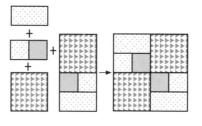

Block B
Make 24.

Baby Crown Jewels

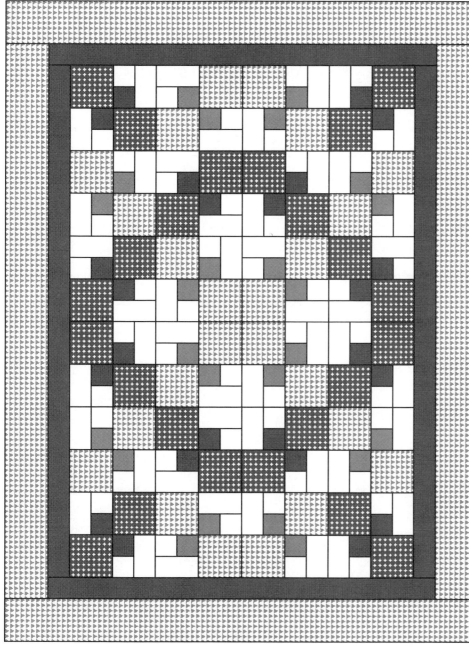

Quilt Plan

Materials: 44"-wide fabric

1 yd. white print or solid for background
⅔ yd. black print
¼ yd. red print or solid
⅔ yd. yellow print
¼ yd. dark blue print or solid
1 yd. red print or solid for inner border and binding
¾ yd. yellow print for outer border
3½ yds. for backing
48" x 64" piece of batting

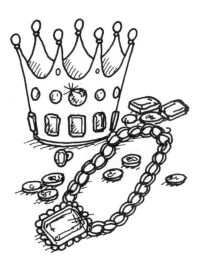

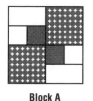

Block A
Make 13.

Block B
Make 13.

Note: Make 13 Block A and 13 Block B. That way, you will have 2 extra blocks to play with if you want to try block arrangements other than the one shown, which only uses 24 blocks. Use the extra blocks in another project or to make a decorative pillow for the rocker in the nursery.

Cutting

Cut the pieces listed in the chart below, cutting all strips across the fabric width (crosswise grain).

| Fabric | First Cut | | Second Cut | |
	No. of Strips	Strip Width	No. of Pieces	Dimensions
Blocks				
White	11*	2½"	52	2½" x 4½"
	*Set aside 4 strips for strip piecing, step 1 below.			
Black	4	4½"	26	4½" square
Red	2	2½"		
Yellow	4	4½"	26	4½" square
Dark blue	2	2½"		
Borders				
Red	4	2½"		
Yellow	5	4½"		

Directions

1. Strip piece 2 units composed of 2½"-wide white and red strips. Crosscut 26 units, each 2½" wide. Repeat with the remaining white strips and the dark blue strips.

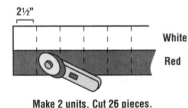

2½"

White

Red

Make 2 units. Cut 26 pieces.

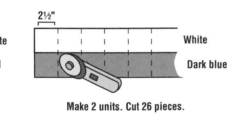

2½"

White

Dark blue

Make 2 units. Cut 26 pieces.

2. Assemble the blocks, following the piecing diagram below. Use black and yellow squares, white rectangles, and the units made in step 1.

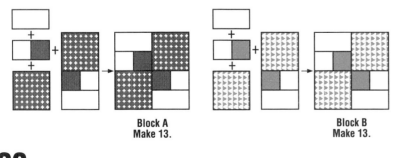

Block A
Make 13.

Block B
Make 13.

3. Referring to the quilt plan on page 65, arrange blocks into horizontal rows. Sew together in rows; then sew rows together.

4. Join the short ends of the red inner border strips to make one long strip. Cut 2 pieces, each 48½" long, for the side borders, and 2 pieces, each 36½" long, for the top and bottom borders. Sew the inner borders to the sides and then to the top and bottom of the quilt top.

5. Join the short ends of the yellow outer border strips to make one long strip. Cut 2 pieces, each 52½" long, for the side borders, and 2 pieces, each 44½" long, for the top and bottom borders. Sew the outer borders to the sides and then to the top and bottom of the quilt top.

6. Layer the finished quilt top with batting and backing.

7. Pin, baste, quilt, and bind, following the quilt finishing directions that begin on page 12.

Dream Wardrobe-Girl

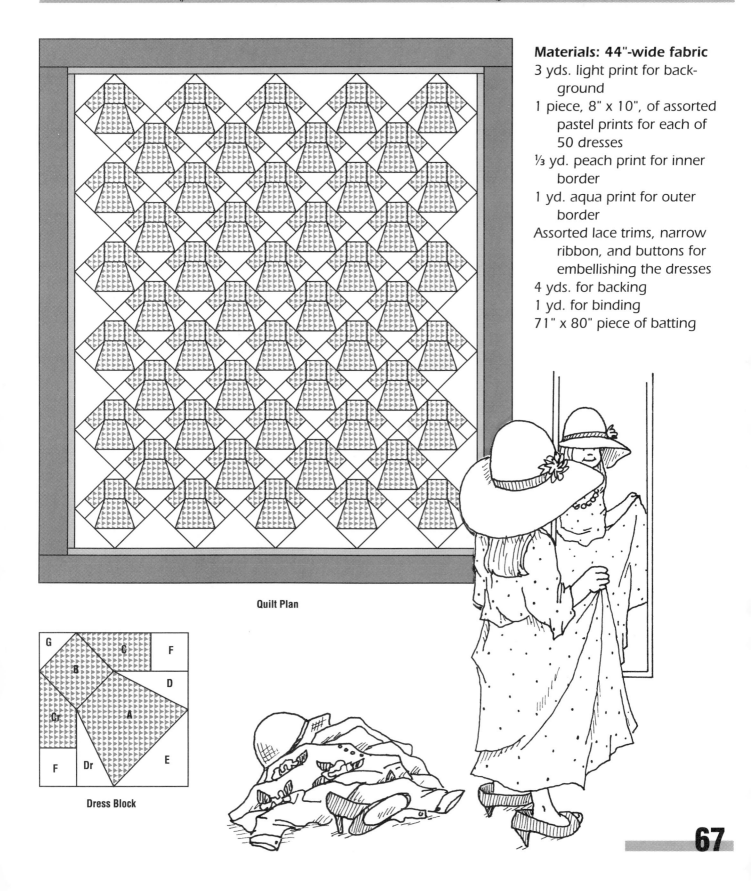

Materials: 44"-wide fabric

3 yds. light print for background

1 piece, 8" x 10", of assorted pastel prints for each of 50 dresses

⅓ yd. peach print for inner border

1 yd. aqua print for outer border

Assorted lace trims, narrow ribbon, and buttons for embellishing the dresses

4 yds. for backing

1 yd. for binding

71" x 80" piece of batting

Quilt Plan

Dress Block

Cutting

Use templates on pages 72–73.

1. From each dress fabric, cut:
   - 1 Template A
   - 1 square, 3¼" x 3¼", for B
   - 1 Template C and 1 Cr

2. Cut the pieces listed in the chart below, cutting all strips across the fabric width (crosswise grain). Some pieces require only one cut, some as many as three.

Fabric	First Cut No. of Strips	First Cut Strip Width	Second Cut No. of Pieces	Second Cut Dimensions	Third Cut No. of Triangles
Blocks and Setting Triangles					
Background print	4	5"	50	Template D	
			50	Template Dr	
	4	5"	25	5" square	◻ 50 for E
	7	2½"	100	2½" square for F	
	3	3"	25	3" square	◻ 50 for G
	2	13"	5	13" square	⊠ 18 for sides
			2	9" square	◻ 4 for corners
Borders					
Peach print	6	1½"			
Aqua print	7	4½"			

◻ = Cut once diagonally to yield half-square triangles.

⊠ = Cut twice diagonally to yield quarter-square triangles.

Directions

1. Arrange the pieces for each block, following the block diagram above, and then decide how you will trim each one. Refer to the quilt photo on page 43 for ideas. Attach trims to the individual pieces before assembling the blocks so that raw ends will be caught in the piecing seams. Waistline trims may be sewn in place after sewing piece A to piece B, before adding the sleeves (C and Cr). Some sleeve and skirt trims may be sewn after sewing C and F together, or A and E together.

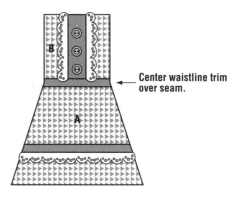

Center waistline trim over seam.

2. Assemble 50 blocks, following the piecing sequence below.

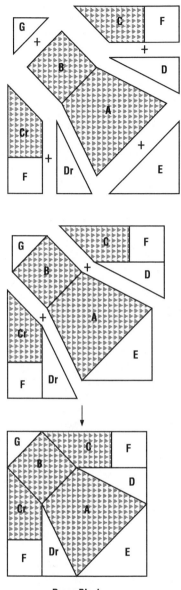

Dress Block
Make 50.

3. Referring to the quilt plan on page 67, arrange blocks with corner and side setting squares. Join in diagonal rows.

4. Join the short ends of the inner border strips to make one long strip. Cut 2 pieces, each 67½" long, for the side borders, and 2 pieces, each 59½" long, for the top and bottom borders. Sew the inner border to the sides and then to the top and bottom of the quilt top.

5. Join the short ends of the outer border strips to make one long strip. Cut 2 pieces, each 69½" long, for the side borders, and 2 pieces, each 67½" long, for the top and bottom borders. Sew the outer border to the sides and then to the top and bottom of the quilt top.

6. Layer the finished quilt top with batting and backing.

7. Pin, baste, quilt, and bind, following the quilt finishing directions that begin on page 12.

Dream Wardrobe—Boy

Quilt Size: 42" x 54"
Block Size: 8"

Materials: 44"-wide fabric

2½ yds. light print for background

1 piece, 6" x 6", for each pair of pants (assorted prints)

1 piece, 7" x 9", for each shirt (assorted prints)

⅔ yd. blue print for setting triangles

¼ yd. red for inner border

¾ yd. light print for outer border

Assorted small buttons for shirts, if desired

2 yds. for backing

⅔ yd. for binding

46" x 58" piece of batting

Quilt Plan

Shirt and Trousers Block

Cutting

Use templates on pages 72–73.

1. For each of 18 pairs of pants, cut 1 and 1r of Template A.
2. For each of 18 shirts, cut:
    1 square, 3¼" x 3¼", for B
    1 and 1r of Template C
    2 squares, each 2" x 2", for collar (I)
3. Cut the pieces listed in the chart below, cutting all strips across the fabric width (crosswise grain). Some pieces require only one cut, some as many as three.

Fabric	First Cut		Second Cut		Third Cut
	No. of Strips	Strip Width	No. of Pieces	Dimensions	No. of Triangles
Blocks					
Background	2	5"	18	Template D	
			18	Template Dr	
	2	5"	9	5" square	◰ 18 for E
	4	2½"	36	2½" x 4" for F	
	1	3"	9	3" square	◰ 18 for G
	2	2"	18	Template H	
Setting Triangles					
Blue print	1	13"	3	13" x 13"	⊠ 10 for sides
			2	8" square	◰ 4 for corners
Borders					
Red	4	1½"			
Light print	5	3½"			

◰ = Cut once diagonally to yield half-square triangles.

⊠ = Cut twice diagonally to yield quarter-square triangles.

Directions

1. Arrange the pieces for each block, following the block diagram at left.
2. To make the collars for each shirt, fold each square (I) in half on the diagonal and then in half again. Position at the top edge of each shirt (B) and pin in place.

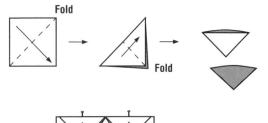

3. Assemble 18 blocks, following the piecing diagram below.

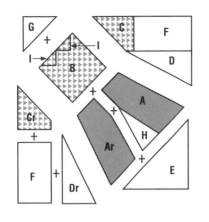

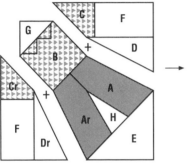

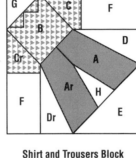

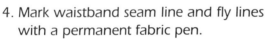

**Shirt and Trousers Block
Make 18.**

**Mark fly and
waistband seam line.**

4. Mark waistband seam line and fly lines with a permanent fabric pen.
5. Referring to the quilt plan on page 70, arrange blocks and setting triangles; then sew together in diagonal rows.
6. Join the short ends of the red inner border strips to make one long strip. Cut 2 pieces, each 44½" long, for the side borders, and 2 pieces, each 36½"long, for the top and bottom borders. Sew the inner borders to the sides and then to the top and bottom of the quilt top.
7. Join the short ends of the light print outer border strips to make one long strip. Cut 2 pieces, each 48½" long, for the side borders, and 2 pieces, each 42½" long, for the top and bottom borders. Sew the outer borders to the sides and then to the top and bottom of the quilt top.
8. Layer the finished quilt top with batting and backing.
9. Pin, baste, quilt, and bind, following the quilt finishing directions that begin on page 12.

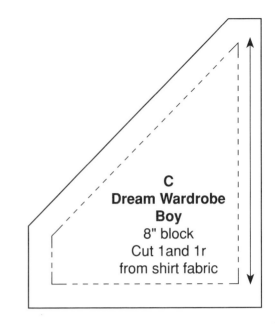

**C
Dream Wardrobe
Boy**
8" block
Cut 1and 1r
from shirt fabric

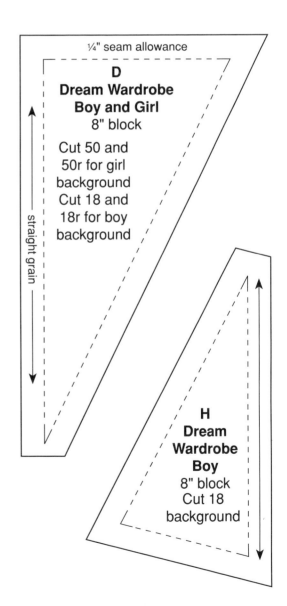

¼" seam allowance

**D
Dream Wardrobe
Boy and Girl**
8" block

Cut 50 and 50r for girl background
Cut 18 and 18r for boy background

straight grain

**H
Dream
Wardrobe
Boy**
8" block
Cut 18
background

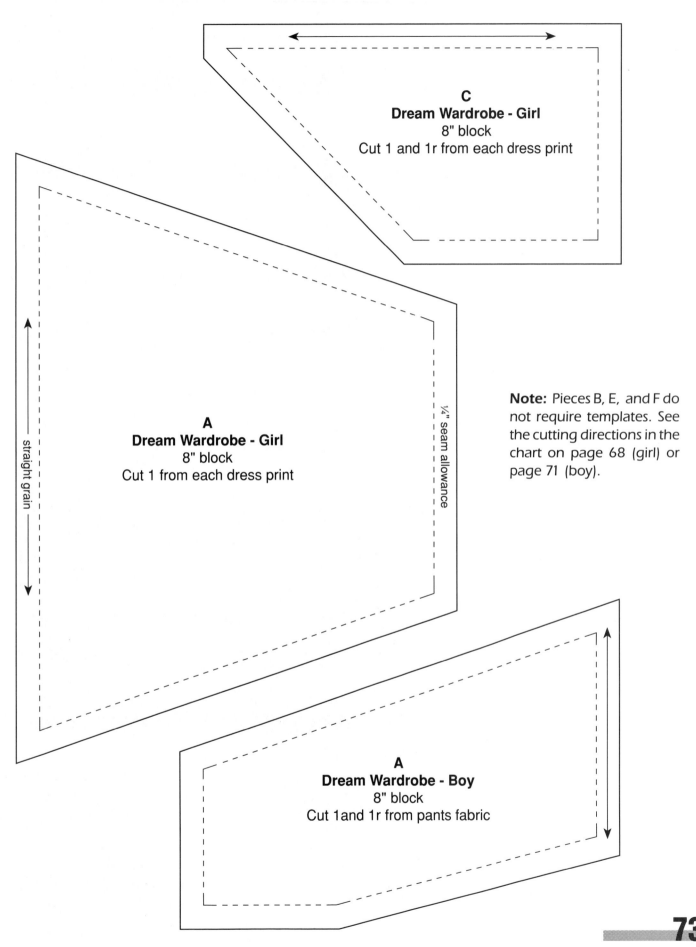

C
Dream Wardrobe - Girl
8" block
Cut 1 and 1r from each dress print

A
Dream Wardrobe - Girl
8" block
Cut 1 from each dress print

straight grain

¼" seam allowance

Note: Pieces B, E, and F do not require templates. See the cutting directions in the chart on page 68 (girl) or page 71 (boy).

A
Dream Wardrobe - Boy
8" block
Cut 1 and 1r from pants fabric

Quilt size: 72" x 88"
Block size: 8"

Materials: 44"-wide fabric

2¼ yds. light green water print for block back-grounds

2½ yds. fish print for inner, middle, and outer bor-ders*

60 pieces of assorted green prints, each 7" x 10", for frogs

1 yd. fabric with large black dots on a white back-ground for eyes (Dots should be at least 1" in diameter.)

5½ yds. for backing

1 yd. for binding

76" x 92" piece of batting

*The cutting directions for the borders are written for fabric that has a definite directional underwater scene. If you use an allover water print with-out direction, you can cut all strips across the width of the fabric. You will need to cut a total of 17 strips; then piece together and cut the border lengths required as listed below. You will need 2¼ yards of fabric for borders cut in this manner.

Quilt Plan

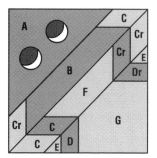

Frog Block

Cutting

Use templates on page 79.

1. From each frog fabric, cut:
   1 square, 6⅞" x 6⅞". Cut once diagonally and set 1 resulting triangle aside for A. From the remaining triangle, cut a 1⅞"-wide strip from the long edge for B. Discard the resulting small triangle.

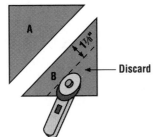

Fold the remaining piece of the frog fabric in half and cut the following:
   1 C and 1 Cr
   1 D and 1 Dr

2. From the fish print for the borders, cut the following strips from the length of the fabric:

2 strips, each 4½" x 80½", for the outer side borders
2 strips, each 4½" x 56½", for the middle side borders
2 strips, each 4½" x 32½", for the inner side borders

From the remaining border fabric, cut enough 4½"-wide strips across the fabric width to total 330". Join the short ends of the strips to make one long strip. Cut the following:
   2 pieces, each 88½" long, for the outer top and bottom borders
   2 pieces, each 48½" long, for the middle top and bottom borders
   2 pieces, each 24½" long, for the inner top and bottom borders

3. Cut the pieces listed in the chart below, cutting all strips across the fabric width (crosswise grain). Some pieces require only one cut, some as many as three.

Fabric	First Cut		Second Cut		Third Cut
	No. of Strips	Strip Width	No. of Pieces	Dimensions	No. of Triangles
Blocks					
Green background	18	1½"	120	Template C	
			120	Template Cr	
	7	4½"	60	4½" square*	
*Position cutting template in one corner and cut corner off. Discard corner. The piece remaining is G.					
	12	1⅞"	60	1⅞" square	◻ 120 for E
			60	Template F	

◻ = Cut once diagonally to yield half-square triangles.

Directions

Blocks

1. Make 60 frog blocks, following the piecing diagram below and sewing the pieces together in diagonal rows. Then sew the rows together, taking care when stitching the bias edges together.

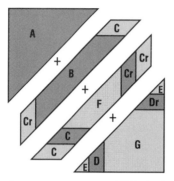

2. From heavy paper, cut 120 circles, using the frog eye template. To cut the frog eyes, position a paper circle on a dot so that the dot is off-center and white shows around approximately half of the circle. Cut out, adding ¼" allowance all around. Cut out 120 eyes.

3. Appliqué eyes on each frog block.

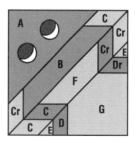

Quilt Top Assembly and Finishing

Refer to the quilt plan on page 74.

1. Arrange the central panel of frogs (4 rows of 2 frogs each). Add inner side borders, then top and bottom borders to the panel.
2. Arrange 2 sets of 5 frogs each in vertical rows with noses pointing toward the central panel. Sew blocks together and then sew to the sides of the inner border.
3. Arrange 2 sets of 5 frogs each in horizontal rows. Sew blocks together in rows; then sew to the top and bottom edges of the inner border. Add the middle border to the sides and then to the top and bottom of the quilt top.
4. Arrange 2 sets of 8 frogs each in vertical rows. Sew blocks together in rows; then sew to the sides of the middle border.
5. Arrange 2 sets of 8 frogs each in horizontal rows. Sew the blocks together in rows; then sew to the top and bottom of the middle border.
6. Sew the outer borders to the sides and then to the top and bottom of the quilt top.
7. Layer the finished quilt top with batting and backing.
8. Pin, baste, quilt, and bind, following the quilt finishing directions that begin on page 12.

Baby Frog Pond

Quilt Plan

Baby Frog Block

Materials: 44"-wide fabric

- 1¼ yds. light green water print for block backgrounds
- 1¼ yds. fish print for inner, middle, and outer borders*
- 28 pieces of assorted green prints, each 7" x 10", for frogs
- ½ yd. fabric with large black dots on a white background for eyes (Dots should be at least 1" in diameter.)
- 4 yds. for backing
- ½ yd. for binding
- 52" x 68" piece of batting

*The cutting directions for the borders are written for fabric that has a definite directional underwater scene. If you use an allover water print without direction, you can cut all strips across the width of the fabric. Cut a total of 9 strips, each 4½" wide.

Cutting
Use templates on page 79.

1. From each frog fabric, cut:
   1 square, 6⅞" x 6⅞". Cut once diagonally and set 1 resulting triangle aside for A. From the remaining triangle, cut a 1⅞"-wide strip from the long edge for B.

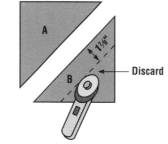

Discard the resulting small triangle. Fold the remaining piece of the frog fabric in half and cut the following:
   1 C and 1 Cr
   1 D and 1 Dr

2. Cut the pieces listed in the chart below, cutting all strips across the fabric width (crosswise grain), except for the border strips, which must be cut from the length of the fabric. Some pieces require only one cut, some as many as three.

Fabric	First Cut		Second Cut		Third Cut
	No. of Strips	Strip Width	No. of Pieces	Dimensions	No. of Triangles
Green background	7	1½"	56	Template C	
			56	Template Cr	
	4	4½"	28	4½" square*	
	* Position cutting template in one corner and cut corner off. Discard corner. The piece remaining is G.				
	6	1⅞"	28	1⅞" square	◹ 56 for E
			28	Template F	
Fish print	9	4½"**			
	** Cut from the lengthwise grain of a directional print or cut on the crosswise grain of an allover print.				
◹ = Cut once diagonally to yield half-square triangles.					

Directions

1. Make 28 frog blocks, following the block assembly directions for the larger quilt on page 76. Cut and prepare 56 eyes as directed and appliqué to the finished blocks.
2. Join the short ends of the border strips to make one long strip. For the inner borders, cut 2 pieces, each 32½" long, for the sides, and 2 pieces, each 24½" long, for the top and bottom borders.
3. For the outer border, cut 2 pieces, each 56½" long, for the sides, and 2 pieces, each 48½" long, for the top and bottom borders.
4. Arrange the central panel of frogs (4 rows of 2 frogs each). Refer to the quilt plan on page 77. Add inner side borders, then top and bottom borders to the panel.
5. Arrange 2 sets of 5 frogs each in vertical rows with noses pointing up toward the central panel. Sew blocks together and then sew to the sides of the inner border.
6. Arrange 2 sets of 5 frogs each in horizontal rows. Sew blocks together into rows; then sew to the top and bottom edges of the inner border. Add the outer borders to the sides and then to the top and bottom of the quilt top.
7. Layer the finished quilt top with batting and backing.
8. Pin, baste, quilt, and bind, following the quilt finishing directions that begin on page 12.

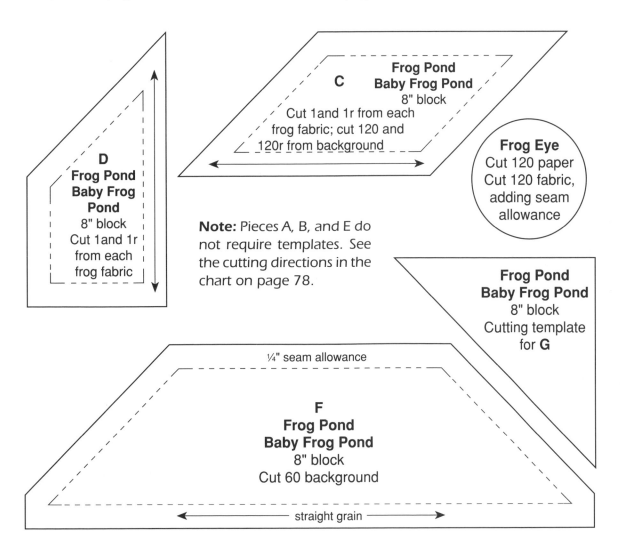

C
Frog Pond
Baby Frog Pond
8" block
Cut 1and 1r from each frog fabric; cut 120 and 120r from background

D
Frog Pond
Baby Frog Pond
8" block
Cut 1and 1r from each frog fabric

Frog Eye
Cut 120 paper
Cut 120 fabric, adding seam allowance

Note: Pieces A, B, and E do not require templates. See the cutting directions in the chart on page 78.

Frog Pond
Baby Frog Pond
8" block
Cutting template for **G**

¼" seam allowance

F
Frog Pond
Baby Frog Pond
8" block
Cut 60 background

straight grain

That Patchwork Place Publications and Products

BOOKS

Angelsong by Joan Vibert
Angle Antics by Mary Hickey
Animas Quilts by Jackie Robinson
Appliqué Borders: An Added Grace by Jeana Kimball
Back to Square One by Nancy J. Martin
Baltimore Bouquets by Mimi Dietrich
A Banner Year by Nancy J. Martin
Basket Garden by Mary Hickey
Blockbuster Quilts by Margaret J. Miller
Calendar Quilts by Joan Hanson
Cathedral Window: A Fresh Look by Nancy J. Martin
Copy Art for Quilters by Nancy J. Martin
Corners in the Cabin by Paulette Peters
Country Threads by Connie Tesene and Mary Tendall
Even More by Trudie Hughes
Fantasy Flowers: Pieced Flowers for Quilters
    by Doreen Cronkite Burbank
Feathered Star Sampler by Marsha McCloskey
Fit To Be Tied by Judy Hopkins
Five- and Seven-Patch Blocks & Quilts for the ScrapSaver™
    by Judy Hopkins
Four-Patch Blocks & Quilts for the ScrapSaver™
    by Judy Hopkins
Go Wild with Quilts: 14 North American Birds and Animals
    by Margaret Rolfe
Handmade Quilts by Mimi Dietrich
Happy Endings—Finishing the Edges of Your Quilt
    by Mimi Dietrich
Holiday Happenings by Christal Carter
Home for Christmas by Nancy J. Martin and Sharon Stanley
In The Beginning by Sharon Evans Yenter
Jacket Jazz by Judy Murrah
Lessons in Machine Piecing by Marsha McCloskey
Little By Little: Quilts in Miniature by Mary Hickey
Little Quilts by Alice Berg, Sylvia Johnson and
    Mary Ellen von Holt
Lively Little Logs by Donna McConnell
Loving Stitches: A Guide to Fine Hand Quilting
    by Jeana Kimball
More Template-Free™ *Quiltmaking* by Trudie Hughes
My Mother's Quilts: Designs from the Thirties
    by Sara Nephew
Nifty Ninepatches by Carolann M. Palmer
Nine-Patch Blocks & Quilts for the ScrapSaver™
    by Judy Hopkins
Not Just Quilts by Jo Parrott
Ocean Waves by Marsha McCloskey and Nancy J. Martin
One-of-a-Kind Quilts by Judy Hopkins
On to Square Two by Marsha McCloskey
Osage County Quilt Factory by Virginia Robertson
Painless Borders by Sally Schneider

A Perfect Match: A Guide to Precise Machine Piecing
    by Donna Lynn Thomas
Picture Perfect Patchwork by Naomi Norman
Pineapple Passion by Nancy Smith and Lynda Milligan
A Pioneer Doll and Her Quilts by Mary Hickey
Pioneer Storybook Quilts by Mary Hickey
Quick & Easy Quiltmaking: 26 Projects Featuring Speedy
    Cutting and Piecing Methods by Mary Hickey,
    Nancy J. Martin, Marsha McCloskey & Sara Nephew
Quilts for All Seasons: Year-Round Log Cabin Designs
    by Christal Carter
Quilts for Kids by Carolann M. Palmer
Quilts from Nature by Joan Colvin
Quilts to Share by Janet Kime
Red and Green: An Appliqué Tradition by Jeana Kimball
Red Wagon Originals by Gerry Kimmel and Linda Brannock
Reflections of Baltimore by Jeana Kimball
Rotary Riot: 40 Fast and Fabulous Quilts by Judy Hopkins
    and Nancy J. Martin
Scrap Happy by Sally Schneider
Sensational Settings: Over 80 Ways to Arrange Your Quilt
    Blocks by Joan Hanson
Sewing on the Line: Fast and Easy Foundation Piecing
    by Lesly-Claire Greenberg
Shortcuts: A Concise Guide to Metric Rotary Cutting
    by Donna Lynn Thomas
Shortcuts: A Concise Guide to Rotary Cutting
    by Donna Lynn Thomas
Small Talk by Donna Lynn Thomas
Smoothstitch™ *Quilts: Easy Machine Appliqué*
    by Roxi Eppler
Stars and Stepping Stones by Marsha McCloskey
The Stitchin' Post by Jean Wells and Lawry Thorn
Strips That Sizzle by Margaret J. Miller
Tea Party Time: Romantic Quilts and Tasty Tidbits
    by Nancy J. Martin
Template-Free™ *Quiltmaking* by Trudie Hughes
Template-Free™ *Quilts and Borders* by Trudie Hughes
Template-Free® *Stars* by Jo Parrott
Threads of Time by Nancy J. Martin
Watercolor Quilts by Pat Maixner Magaret and
    Donna Ingram Slusser
Women and Their Quilts by Nancyann Johanson Twelker

TOOLS

6" Bias Square®
8" Bias Square®
Metric Bias Square®
BiRangle™
Pineapple Rule

Rotary Mate™
Rotary Rule™
Ruby Beholder™
ScrapSaver™

VIDEO

Shortcuts to America's Best-Loved Quilts

Many titles are available at your local quilt shop. For more information, send $2 for a color catalog to That Patchwork Place, Inc., PO Box 118, Bothell WA 98041-0118 USA.

☎ Call 1-800-426-3126 for the name and location of the quilt shop nearest you.